Love is the Message that I Heard

Love's the Message that I Heard

Msgr. Bob Guste

Foreword by Archbishop Phillip M. Hannan

PUBLISHING COMPANY
P.O. Box 220 • Goleta, CA 93116
(800) 647-9882 • (805) 692-0043 • Fax: (805) 967-5133

Nihil Opstat: Reverend Dennis H. Hayes, III
                Censor Librorum

Imprimatur: Most Reverend Alfred C. Hughes
                Archbishop of New Orleans

September 3, 2002

Almost all Biblical passages are from the revised edition of the New American Bible, copyright 1985, by Confraternity of Christian Doctrine, Washington, D.C. When either the unrevised edition (copyright 1970, CCD) or another version is used it will be indicated in the text.

All Vatican Council II statements are taken from *Documents of the Vatican II*, (American Press/Association Press 1966). Walter M. Abbott, S.J., general editor.

Words bold-faced from Scripture and other quotations indicate emphasis added.

The "Portrait of Jesus" by Richard Hook on page 53 is used with permission. Copyright by Concordia Publishing House. The picture "Our Lady of the Millennium" on page 84 is likewise used with permission. Copyright by John Brandi Co.

© 2002 Queenship Publishing - All Rights Reserved.

Library of Congress Number # 2002095725

Published by:
    Queenship Publishing
    P.O. Box 220
    Goleta, CA 93116
    (800) 647-9882 • (805) 692-0043 • Fax: (805) 967-5133

Printed in the United States of America

ISBN: 1-57918-224-0

TABLE OF CONTENTS

I   The God We Don't Believe In *Page 1*
Who is our Father?
1.) Five False Images of God 2.) The Man Upstairs 3.) Limited Like Us 4.) A Traffic Cop 5.) Santa Claus 6.) Sad Sadie 7.) The God Who Is 8.) God Reveals Himself 9.) Finally Through Jesus 10.) Abba, Papa, Daddy 11.) God Likes You 12.) Tough Love 13.) Unconditional Love 14.) Response of Sons and Daughters 15.) Trustful 16.) Thankful 17.) Thoughtful

II Who Is Jesus Christ? *Page 29*
The difference between knowing about and knowing
1.) One Solitary Life 2.) By Faith: Messiah 3.) Savior 4.) Our Lord and Our God 5.) Who is Jesus for You? 6.) Jesus at the Center of the Church 7.) My Brother, Friend, and Bridegroom 8.) My Savior 9.) Jesus Christ is Lord

III The Prayer That Pierces The Clouds And Hearts *Page 55*
How's and why's of personal and communal prayer
  Part I Personal Prayer
  1.) So Why Pray? 2.) From the Heart 3.) Five Aspects of Prayer 4.) Practices of Prayer 5.) Meditative Prayer 6.) Using Quiet Time 7.) Listening in Prayer 8.) Five Antennae for Prayer 9.) A Quieting Technique
  Part II Community and Shared Prayer
  1.) Prayer Groups 2.) The Liturgy 3.) The Mass 4.) His Sacrifice and Ours 5.) His Love Communicated and Celebrated 7.) Give It All You've Got 8.) A Prayer About Prayer

Continued on next page

IV The Gift Of His Church   *Page 85*
Your part today in the mission of Jesus
Part I Why the Church and what is my mission in her?
1.) Why Do We Need the Church? 2.) Expressing the Mystery 3.) Spots, Wrinkles, Scandals 4.) The Body's Head 5.) A Body Needs Members 6.) Our Mission as Members of the Body 7.) Evangelization 8.) Being Witnesses
Part II Unity and Reconciliation A body has to be together
1.) Unity in Faith 2.) Unity and Morality 3.) Catholics and Contraception 4.) Together in Love 5.) Prayer 6.) The Sacrament of Reconciliation—putting flesh on His Forgiveness 7.) Overcoming Fear 8.) Examination of Conscience

V Mission Impossible Made Possible   *Page 121*
The Holy Spirit
1.) Why Do We Need the Holy Spirit? 2.) The Holy Spirit in the Old and New Testaments 3.) You Will Be Witnesses 4.) Comic Relief and Direction 5.) Awareness of the Spirit 6.) Surrendering to the Spirit 7.) Prayer

Appendix
Prayer for the Inner Healing of Memories   *Page 139*

About the Author   *Page 143*

DEDICATION

to

Teresa

A faithful self-sacrificing secretary

and to

her husband "Buddy" and daughter Lisa

and all

who like them for years have volunteered prayer, sacrifice, encouragement, witness and work in the exciting and loving mission of proclaiming the Good News.

FOREWORD

In his book entitled Love's the Message that I Heard, Monsignor Guste goes right to the heart of the matter—our union with the Persons of the Holy Trinity. He deals directly with our relationship with God the Father, God the Son and His human nature, Jesus Christ, and the Holy Spirit.

This book deals with our fulfillment of the basic command that Christ gave to us, *"Go, therefore,* and teach all the nations, *baptizing them in the name of the Father and of the Son and of the Holy Spirit."* (Mt 28:19-20) Our troubles, in the Church and in the world, derive from our neglect of this primary task and our preoccupation with the secondary or subsidiary matters. It provides the correct perspective for the arguments or discussions about the composition of the Parish Council, selection of the chairperson for parish organization, participation of the laity in the financial affairs of the parish and diocese, the conduct of the parish school, activities for the youth, ordination of women, etc.

Where there is centrality of attention on Jesus Christ there is a development of unity of Christians with Jesus, the flowering of the Spirit announced by St. Paul, *"I live, no longer I, but Christ lives in me."* (Gal 2:20) This flowering enables us to perform our duties in an intensity and precision that lifts us to the level of seeing all things in the light of Christ. It applies to our growing into the *"full stature of Christ"* (Gal 4:13) and thus affecting the solution of the deep problems of our times. Living with Christ in the manner described in this book enables us to achieve the enormous goal and challenge of Jesus, as expressed by St. Paul: *"This may be a wicked age, but your lives should redeem it."* (Eph 5:16 The Jersualem Bible) We can achieve this end by conforming ourselves to Christ.

"For we are Is handiwork, created in Christ Jesus for the good works that God has prepared in advance, that we should live in them." (Eph 2:10)

Most Rev. Phillip Hannan
Former Archbishop of New Orleans
President, Focus Worldwide Television Network.

INTRODUCTION

What is your image of God? What is God really like? How can we know? (Many who say they believe in God have all kinds of false and distorted images of Him. Many who say they don't believe may only be rejecting these images.) What does it mean when we call Him Father?

Who is Jesus Christ? What is His place in the history of the human race? What is your relationship with Him? Do you know Him as a brother and friend, as your Savior and Lord? Do you walk through life with the risen Lord, sharing your joys and sorrows with Him? Do you experience His saving and transforming grace daily at work within you? Do you turn everything over to Him and say, "Jesus, show me what you want me to do with it all—and just use me."

How do you pray? Why pray if you often don't get what you ask for? What is the main purpose of prayer anyway? Do you pray *from the heart* or just the lips? In prayer do you do all the talking or do you ever *listen*? Do you believe He wants to talk to you in the quiet of your heart—more than you want to talk to Him?

Do you regularly pray with others, husband and wife, parents and children, friend and friend—not just formal prayer but spontaneous as well? What about the great community prayers of the Church—the Liturgy of the Hours and the sacraments? What about the Holy Eucharist? Are you awestruck and deeply moved by the thought of going to Mass, as moved as you would be if you lived in Jerusalem at the time of Jesus and one day discovered under your door an invitation to that supper with Him the night before He died?

What about the Catholic Church? If you're a member, are you excited about that? When is the last time you got down on your knees and thanked God that through no merit of your own, He called you into membership in His body the Church? Do you realize that you belong to the Church that goes back two thousand years in an unbroken line to Jesus, Peter and the apostles? Do you know that in that Church, with all the weaknesses we exhibit as members, Jesus Christ has left us the visible instrument through which *His own mission is continued*, until the end of time? Does that turn you on? Do you want to tell the whole world the good news about the Lord and His Church, sharing with others all He has shared with you? Do you know how to accomplish this mission?

What about the Holy Spirit? Do you realize that the same Holy Spirit who was given to Peter and the apostles to begin the work of the Church is offered to you today to continue that mission? Are you aware of the presence and power of the Spirit in your everyday life—enlightening, guiding, strengthening, and consoling you? Do you know that at the beginning of the Second Vatican Council, Pope John XXIII prayed that in this our day there would be a new Pentecost, and that our present Pope (John Paul II) has prayed for the same, calling it a "new springtime of Christian life...if Christians are docile to the action of the Holy Spirit"? Do you realize that you're called to be a part of that new springtime as you become daily more aware of the Holy Spirit dwelling within you, and surrender to Him more and more?

Those questions addressed here and the experiences shared—mine and others—are those of a lifetime. A particular experience happened maybe thirty years ago when I made a private retreat at Madonna House, about one hundred miles north of Toronto.

A unique feature of this spiritual center is that in addition to the community houses, there are hermitages, or "poustinias," in the hills which are available to Madonna House members or visitors. The rules for using these austere places of prayer and solitude are that you bring with you nothing more than a loaf of bread, a jug of water, and a Bible.

I went out one morning, intending to spend the day and come back the next. After checking out the hermitage, with its simple table, oil lamp, wood stove, and cot, I spend the day walking and meditating in the hills. My prayer was for guidance: "Lord, what do you want me to do with my life as a priest different from what I'm already doing? What changes do you want me to make? What do you want me to put in or leave out?"

There were some things that came to mind. I wrote them down at the time but no longer remember them. What I do remember is that, as the sun began to go down in the hills, I could hear the Lord speak to me silently in the quiet of my heart. It went something like this:

"Hey, Bob, you're doing the wrong thing. You're spending all your time thinking of *your* work, your life, and your plans. That's okay, but it's not the main reason I brought you out to these hills. I brought you here primarily to think of **Me**. I want you to let sink into your mind and heart what it really means when you say God is your Father—how I hold you in the palm of my hand, call you by name, and love you as if you were my only child. I want you to let sink in what it means that the eternal Son of God became man and was born into this world out of love for you, and that He is now your brother, your Savior, and Lord of your life. I want you to let sink in the mystery of the Holy Spirit, who dwells in your heart to lead and guide, lift up, inspire, and move you along day by day to continue the mission of Jesus."

"I also want you to open your heart anew to the gift of Mary, the Mother of Jesus, given to you as your spiritual Mother to assist you along the way in following her Son. Let all this sink in *first*, and the rest will follow: you'll know what I want you to do."

When I got back to the cabin, it was already dark. I lit the oil lamp at the desk and opened the Bible to read the first thing my eyes would fall upon: *A leper came to him (and kneeling down) begged him and said, 'If you wish, you can make me clean,' Moved with pity, he stretched out his hand, touched him, and said to him, 'I do will it. Be made clean.' The leprosy left him immediately, and he was made clean."* (Mk1:40-42)

All alone in the cabin that night, I began to say over and over to Jesus, "Lord, if you wish to do so, you can heal me." I wasn't sure what I meant, but it was something like this: "You can win the daily battle over sin in my life. You can take the blinders off my eyes and the defenses from my heart to let in your love. You can make me free and open to all you want to say to me and do in and through me." As I repeated the prayer over and over, it was as if He were responding. "*I do will it*; be healed."

It was a couple of years after this experience that I began to do some parish mission revivals using the basic theme of Father, Son, and Holy Spirit. Each night of the mission is devoted to a different person of the Trinity, with a night on prayer and another on commitment tothe Church and Reconciliation.

A valiant woman, working from a wheelchair and using two pencils to type because her hands are also crippled, was willing to transcribe these talks from cassettes and then help me painstakingly rework them for publication. What I'm sharing with you is what has touched my life and helped me and others. I pray that something in these pages may be a blessing for you.

Our Lady of the Rosary

October 7, 2002

CHAPTER 1

The God We Don't Believe In
Who is Our Father?

"No one knows the Son except the Father, and no one knows the Father except the Son and anyone to whom the Son wishes to reveal him" (Mt II:27). Please, Lord Jesus, as life goes along, reveal the Father to me more and more.

At the end of a mission I preached in Tupelo, Mississippi, an elderly couple presented me with a little paperback book entitled, *God, Man, and Archie Bunker*. (Archie is the main character in the TV comedy series "All in the Family.") I never read the whole book, but it highlights Archie's unique concept or image of God. Believe it or not, Archie is a believer—as far as God's existence is concerned. What kind of God he believes in is another question!

Archie's god (like Archie) is white, prejudiced, narrow-minded, and bigoted! Now his son-in-law "Meat-head" doesn't believe in God. "Meat-head," on the other hand, is considerate, compassionate, broad-minded, and tolerant. When "Meat-head" looks at Archie, is there any wonder why he doesn't believe?

What is your image of God? How do you picture Him? Sure, God is pure spirit, but we still find ourselves conjuring up images in our imaginations when we think of Him. These images might either be helpful or harmful. False images can do immeasurable harm in our relationship with Him. I know this from my own experience and that of others. Many who reject God completely do not realize that, at heart, they may be rejecting not Him but distorted images of Him, which enlightened believers also reject. On the other hand, many believers who accept God are hampered in their relationship with Him or fail to deepen that relationship or let it have its proper impact on their lives because of improper or deficient images of Him. Let me mention what I would consider just five false images, contrasting each with a more authentic Judeo-Christian image.

THE MAN UPSTAIRS

Have you ever heard about "the man upstairs?" Who hasn't? Sure it's used with humor, but it helps perpetuate a widespread misrepresentation of God. What do you picture when you hear that expression—someone way upstairs, a million miles away, out of reach for us earthbound critters? Is that true of God? The Bible says, *"In Him we live and move and have our being"* (Acts 17:28). The old song, "He's Got the Whole World in His Hands" captures that truth. "He's got you and me brother...you and me sister...the little tiny baby...in His hands." God is closer to you than the air you breathe or the skin on your body. This very moment, He's holding you in the palm of His invisible, almighty "hand." If it weren't for Him, you would vanish from the face of the earth this instant. Puff! You would just go out of existence. When something is created out of nothing, it goes back into nothing unless the one who created it continues to *sustain it in being every single moment*—as God is doing this moment for you. *"You indeed are my help, and in the shadow of your wings I shout for joy. My soul clings fast to you; your right hand upholds me"* (Ps 63:8-9).

LIMITED LIKE US

What else do you picture when you hear "the man upstairs?" Do you picture a man who is powerful but still limited in some way like all of us human beings and who every now and then intervenes in our affairs? What a supremely diminished image of God! The very difference between God and us is that **He is unlimited and all-mighty.** He's not a superman. He is the divine, eternal, infinite, spirit being—the ultimate source and sustainer of all that is.

It's true that God did come among us in human form 2000 years ago in the person of Jesus Christ of Nazareth. God the Son, who is eternally one with the Father and the Holy Spirit—without ceasing to be God—joined Himself to our human nature in the womb of the Blessed Virgin Mary and was born among us. In

Him, the human and divine natures were forever united. Now and eternally, God **in His own divine nature** is not a man but a spirit—a spirit who is infinitely powerful, wise, and good.

For example, consider the vastness of our universe. We reside on only one of its small planets. Look up at the sky on a clear night. How many stars can you see? It would be about two thousand. Astronomers now know that, for every star we see with the naked eye, there are countless stars we can't see. With large telescopes, we can photograph over thirty billion stars, and there must be billions more beyond them. And their size? Of those photographed, most are bigger than our sun, which is one-hundred-nine times the diameter of the earth. It is now said that there are as many stars as grains of sand on all the seashores of the world!

God told Abraham, *"Look up at the sky and count the stars if you can...I will bless you abundantly and make your descendants as countless as the stars of the sky and the sands of the seashore"* (Gn 15:5 & 22:17). *"When I see the heavens, the work of your fingers, the moon and the stars that you set in place,"* the psalmist cries, *"what are humans that you are mindful of them, mere mortals that you care for them?"* (Ps 8:4-5).

Rightfully we sing the words: "How great thou art...O Lord my God, when I in awesome wonder, consider all the worlds thy hands have made. I see the stars. I hear the rolling thunder; thy power throughout the universe proclaims. Then sings my soul, my Savior God, to Thee, 'How great thou art, how great thou art.'"

A TRAFFIC COP

For some, God is the cop behind the tree ready to catch you when you go over the speed limit. His great preoccupation is with rules and guilt, wrongdoing and punishment. That's another false image of God.

The opposite image is that which emerges from a modern-day parable that's attributable to the English writer and Catholic convert, G. K. Chesterton. There were these children who lived with their families on a high mountain. On the summit was a plateau, a level area, where the children could play freely, running and jumping to their heart's content. For the children's protection, the parents had erected a fence around the edge of the plateau to prevent anyone from falling off.

One evening, under cover of darkness, some of the older children, feeling hemmed in by the fence and resenting parental interference with their freedom, tore the barrier down. The next day, when the children went out to play, there was no running and jumping, no laughing and frolicking about. They were all huddled together in the middle of the plateau, afraid to move freely about lest they fall off the mountain.

God created us out of love to share His life and love now and forever. *"I came so that they might have life and have it more abundantly,"* Jesus said (Jn 10:10). God's laws (natural and revealed) and those of His Church are not meant just to restrict us. They set the limits and guidelines for our human life and activity to protect us. Within those limits, we can live life abundantly and productively, full of meaning, love, and joy. *"I've told you this so that my joy might be in you and your joy might be complete"* (Jn 15:11). That's what God wants for us. So much of the guilt and misery in the human family are the consequences of our own misuse of the freedom He has given—or of our own misperception of the God who made us.

With an automobile comes the operator's manual. If you ignore it in rebellion and put water in the gas tank and gas in the radiator, you'll end up in disaster. The manufacturer knows the correct and best use of his product, and so does the Creator.

SANTA CLAUS

Another false image, opposite of the policeman, is the Santa Claus, goody-goody, or push-over god. God is all sweetness and light, and, with Him, anything goes. "God is good," they say. "He doesn't punish. You just do whatever you think best, honey, or whatever turns you on, and He'll take care of you!"

Where did we ever get that image, as common as it is? None of the prophets nor Jesus Himself ever talked about God that way. For all of them, there is right and there is wrong. They challenge us to make the right choices based on reason and God's revelation and not just on whims and emotions. There are also consequences to our choices—even eternal consequences for good or for ill. *"I have set before you life and death, blessing and curse,"* Moses cried out. *"Choose life, then, that you and your descendants may live..."* (Dt 30:19). Jesus warned, *"These will go off to eternal punishment, but the righteous to eternal life"* (Mt 25:46).

"The greatest sin of our times is the denial of sin itself," said a mid-twentieth century pope, Pius XII. That reality is also what prompted the famous psychiatrist, Karl Menninger, to write the book, *Whatever Happened to Sin?* Yes, God is good. He is good beyond anything you or I could ever express or imagine! But you don't just do whatever you please, think you're okay, and just slide into heaven. *"Make no mistake: God is not mocked, for a person will reap only what he sows"* (Gal 6:7).

SAD SADIE

The last false image of God that I've chosen is God, the Sad Sadie. He never smiles, and we can never please Him. Many people apparently have that image. They don't normally associate joy and happiness, fun, laughter, and acceptance with God and religion. They don't smile that much in the house of the Lord, the church, even though the psalmist sings, *"I rejoiced when I heard them say, 'Let us go up to the house of the Lord!'"* (Ps 122). They never accept God's acceptance of them. You know, it doesn't have to be perfect to please Him. I like the statement (reversing the traditional one) that anything worth doing is worth doing *badly*. Sure, give it your best shot, but most of us can't do a perfect job all the time (if ever), but when our efforts come from a good heart, He smiles or hugs us and says, *"Well done"* (Mt 25:21).

God made us to live as long as He lives—in joy. The happiness of this life is just a foretaste of it. *"Eye has not seen and ear has not heard, nor has it entered into the heart of man what things God has prepared for those who love Him"* (I Cor 2:9). True joy begins now as we open our hearts more and more to the mystery of His love, and it culminates in the fullness of life and love in heaven.

Love's the Message that I Heard

The word "joy" is used almost 200 times in the Bible. "Gospel" itself means "Good News." Check out St. Luke and see all the rejoicing, even in the first two chapters. Read Paul's letter to the Philippians—written from prison—and find joy or rejoicing mentioned fifteen times. God is no Sad Sadie, and He's calling us to joy now and forever.

I think of the foreign missionary, now deceased, who told me of an entire village that came into the Catholic Church. Their joy was so great that at Mass they danced all the way up the aisle to Holy Communion. I'm not recommending that you try that next Sunday in your parish church (dancing in the U.S. might only distract), but, for them, it indicated a completely different image of God.

Well, there you have it—five false images of God. Do you remember them? They are (1) the man upstairs, (2) a superman, but still limited like us, (3) a traffic cop just on the look-out to nab the violator, (4) Santa, the push-over, and (5) Sad-Sadie. All are false gods and idols. So break them. Destroy them. Get rid of them and forget them.

THE GOD WHO IS

Let's now talk about who God really is. But how can we? Well, remember that one way we can talk about God is because the whole world is a reflection of the one who made it. What someone does normally says something about the one who does it. That's true of all of us, and it's true of God.

I love nature as so many do, and the beauties of nature cry out to me about God. *"The heavens declare the glory of God and the firmament proclaims his handiwork"* (Ps 19:2). A sunrise. A sunset. The stars at night. The beauty of flowers. The simplest things. I don't know how anyone can look at even one wildflower and conclude that it's just an accident—and to think that there are thousands of different varieties of flowers and plants! *"Not even Solomon in all his glory was dressed like one of them"* (Lk 12:27). Is there no artist back of that?

Consider the human being. A little child. The wonder of the

The God We Don't Believe In

human organism. The magnificence of what each and every one of us is. The human ear—better than the best telephone. The human eye—better than the best Japanese camera. The human nervous system—better than all the wiring that lights up any of our big cities by night. All of that cries out to me about the wonder, the magnificence, and the wisdom of God! In modern times we've discovered the power of the atom. In just one drop of water, how many atoms are there? One hundred billion billion, scientists say. Inside each atom there is an amazing unseen energy and activity—much like that of our solar system. The electrons swirl constantly around a nucleus at an unbelievable rate of speed. If you split just one of those atoms, it releases tremendous power. Now, think of all the atoms in the world. That's just a little idea of the power of God.

All that wisdom and power, all that is beautiful, good, and true is a reflection of God who is infinite Wisdom and Power, Beauty, Goodness, and Truth itself. All of our inner experiences of unselfish love and joy are also experiences of Him who is perfect joy and perfect love.

GOD REVEALS HIMSELF

Beyond all this, God has personally revealed Himself to us. When you love somebody, you want to communicate with that person. You want to reveal your thoughts, your plans, and your very self.

When I was young, I remember kidding my dad and mom, "I don't know how you two can still be talking to each other so much after all these years. By this time, you should have run out of things to say!" But they never got tired of talking and discovering more and more about one another, because they loved each other (and got aggravated at each other from time to time, as well).

Out of love, God wanted to communicate with us about Himself and His plan for us: why we're here, where we're going, and how to get there. It's the most natural thing in the world that He would do that. And He did. Through the patriarchs, prophets and events of the Old Testament, He prepared the way for the great revelation and communication of Himself in Our Lord and Savior, Jesus Christ. Providentially, much of that revelation was written down under His inspiration (Scripture), and much was also handed down by word of mouth and other ways (Sacred Tradition) from one generation to the next.

I think of the Bible as love letters from Our Father. My earthly father died overseas many years ago. On the ship going over, he wrote me a letter every day. I treasure those letters as a precious gift to me. I think of Sacred Scripture much that way, and I want to read it every day of my life.

FINALLY THROUGH JESUS

The opening words of the New Testament letter to the Hebrews are *"In times past, God spoke in fragmentary and varied ways to our fathers through the prophets; in this the final age, he has spoken to us through his Son, whom he has made heir of all things and through whom he first created the universe.* **This Son is the reflection of the Father's glory, the exact representation of the Father's being...**" (vv 1-3 NAB, unrevised edition). In the Gospel of St. John, on the night before Our Lord gives His life out of love for us and as He is at Supper with his apostles, Philip says to Him, *"Master, show us the Father, and that will be enough for us."* And Jesus replies, *"Have I been with you for so long a time and you still do not know me, Philip?* **Whoever has seen me has seen the Father.** *How can you say, 'Show us the Father'? Do you not believe that I am in the Father and the Father is in me?"* (14:8-10).

Do you realize what Jesus is saying? Do you want to know God? Do you want to see God? Do you want to touch God? Then look at the one whom God has sent—God in the flesh. The eternal Son of God who has taken our human nature is *"the reflection of the Father's glory."* In Him, God has been made visible. *"He is the image of the invisible God"* (Col 1:15). **We can know God now in and through Jesus.**

This is one reason He is called the **Word** of God (Jn 1:1 & 14). The Father expresses Himself eternally in His Son and, in time, speaks to us about Himself through Him. Everything that Jesus

The God We Don't Believe In

did is telling us something about the kind of God that is our God. All the different events in the life of Jesus—His growing up in a little village, working by the sweat of His brow, going to the marriage feast of Cana, taking the children in His arms, forgiving the woman caught in adultery, exposing the hypocrisy of some of the Pharisees, cleansing the temple in Jerusalem, hanging on the cross between heaven and earth—tell us something about who God really is.

Look at Jesus; contemplate Him and see. He's a God who's interested in every detail of our human lives—knowing them not only as God, but also experiencing so much as man. He shared in family life, living in a family for thirty years as a child, a teenager, and a young adult. He experienced our work lives as a carpenter in Nazareth and an intimate companion of the fishermen who became His apostles. He knew in His own home the sanctity and devotion of married life as a son honoring the marriage of Mary and Joseph. He participated in our social lives, spending time interacting with people and celebrating with them as a guest at their tables and at the wedding reception (where He actually performed His first miracle).

He's a God who's so close to every one of us and so tender that He can take little children in his arms, laugh with them, listen to their chatter, and converse with them (Mt 19:13-15). He's a God of mercy who, when we come to Him with humble hearts, is as ready to forgive us as He was to forgive the woman caught in adultery. Confronting the angry mob ready to stone her, Jesus tells them, *"Let the one among you who is without sin be the first to throw a stone at her;"* then He turns to the woman and says, *"Go* (and) *from now on do not sin anymore"* (Jn 8:7&11).

He's a God who sees right through all our pretenses and hypocrisy as he lashes out at some of the religious leaders of His day, calling them *"whitewashed tombs which appear beautiful on the outside, but inside are full of dead men's bones..."* (Mt 23:27). He's a God who wants to cleanse the temples of our hearts and of this world and make of them His dwelling place, as He drove the money changers out of the temple in Jerusalem (Jn 2:13-17). He's a God who loves you and me enough to give his life for every one of us

9

on that cross. That's the kind of God who is our God.

Jesus not only showed God to us by His *actions*; He also taught us about God in *words*. His teachings unveiled the mystery of God's Trinitarian life—a mystery hidden from all eternity and only foreshadowed in the Old Testament. As Pope John Paul expresses it, Jesus revealed that "God in His deepest mystery is not a solitude but a family." Yes, clearly there is only one God, but the one God is Father, Son, and Holy Spirit—one divine nature, but three divine persons (e.g. Mt. 28:19). In God eternally, there is Fatherhood, Sonship, and the Holy Spirit; there is dynamic, total, self-giving love—the essence of family life. Here, we'll concentrate on what Jesus revealed to us about God as Our Father.

ABBA, PAPA, DADDY

Jesus' language was Aramaic, and in Aramaic, the word He used for Father was Abba. It is a warm, familiar, and tender word, like Daddy or Papa. Abba is still used in some languages today. What's the first word that most little children learn? Isn't it Mama, Daddy, or Papa? We don't realize what a disarming and even *revolutionary* thing it was when Jesus taught us that we could call God Abba, or Papa. The Jewish people and the prophets before Him would not even dare to pronounce the name of God. When they learned from Jesus that you can take the first simple word that a little child lisps and that you can apply it to God with childlike affection, closeness, and love—that was revolutionary!

What is Jesus teaching when He uses that simple word? Remember, He said, *"Do not think that I have come to abolish the law or the prophets. I have come, not to abolish, but to fulfill"* (Mt 5:17). Building on everything that had been taught before Him, Jesus is launching us out into new depths of understanding.

In the Old Testament, there are preparations for this revelation of who God is. For example, we find them in the prophet Isaiah. In the 43rd chapter, *"I have called you by name: You are mine. Because you are precious in my eyes and glorious, and because I love you"* (vv 1 & 4). You see, God knows you personally. He calls you by name. You're precious to Him. The prophet Hosea

The God We Don't Believe In

says, "*When Israel was a child, I loved him. Out of Egypt, I called my son. It was I who taught Ephraim to walk, who took them in my arms; I fostered them like one who raises an infant to his cheeks*" (Hosea 11:1-4).

God's love is also reflected in a mother's love. "*Can a mother forget her infant, be without tenderness for the child of her womb? Even should she forget, I will never forget you. See, upon the palms of my hands I have written your name*" (Isaiah 49:15-16). Are you a father or mother, husband or wife, brother, sister, or friend to anyone? Do you know the meaning of love for another?

Well, suppose I could go all over the world right now and reach into the heart of every person who has any love—every father and mother, husband and wife, every brother, sister, and friend. We're all human and we're all sinners, so we never love perfectly. Sometimes, we fail to love at all; we're not thoughtful, or we're even hard-hearted and cruel, but if I could go and extract **whatever genuine love could be found in the hearts of all the people on the face of the earth and put it all together, it would still just be a sample of the love that God has for you and me—every single one of us right now.** That's an amazing truth. I'm not able to comprehend it, and yet, when I say it today, it means more to me than it did 25 years ago or maybe even last year—if not yesterday!

GOD LIKES YOU

God not only loves you; He also **likes** you. Have you ever thought about that? God likes me! God delights in me! That's a realization that, for a long time in my life, I never had, but it began to dawn on me years ago, particularly through words of Scripture. I'd say, "Wow! Is God really saying that to me?"

I remember it was a week-day Mass in my first pastorate, probably the feast of the Transfiguration. On the mountain, the Father's voice is heard calling Jesus my "*beloved Son*" with whom I am "*well pleased*" (Mk 1:11, Lk. 3:22), or saying equivalently "...in you I take delight." I said to the congregation that morning, "When reading those words today, I realize something I didn't realize before. Yes, they refer to Jesus, the only divine Son of God, but they

11

also refer to you and me, *His brothers and sisters, the Father's adopted sons and daughters.* The Father is addressing those words of love and delight to us. I'm aware of this, and I'm sharing it with you—but I don't really believe it. I believe it with my mind but not my heart. If I could ever let it sink into my heart, my guts, and my whole being that the Father is truly saying to me: 'Bob, you are my son. I love you. I delight in you.' Wow! That would be one of the happiest days of my life."

It might have been because I shared this with that little congregation. It might have been because they prayed for me, but I remember that it was on that day that I began to experience something of what it's like to believe with mind and heart that the Father is saying to me, "You are my son, my beloved. In you I take delight." I pray you experience the same.

I'm not good at making things with my hands, but one day in my first parish near the Mississippi River, I took a walk on the levee and picked up two small pieces of driftwood. With them, I made a driftwood cross and put it up in my office. When people would come in, they'd sometimes say, "Man! That must be some special kind of wood. It must be from Jerusalem." "No," I'd answer, "it's just two pieces of sticks out of the Mississippi River." But it was special to me because *I had made it.*

That's the way God looks at you—at each one of us. You're special to Him because He made you. Psalm 139 says, *"You formed my inmost being; you knit me in my mother's womb. I praise you, so wonderfully you made me; wonderful are your works"* (vv 13-14).

Carefully, mysteriously, and lovingly, God formed every one of us over a period of nine months or so, and He made each of us different. There are no two people in the world who are completely the same, physically, emotionally, or mentally. Not even so-called identical twins are exactly alike, because there is always some kind of discernible difference between them.

Being from the deep South, I'm nuts about snow. (It snows in New Orleans about once every ten years!) Those who have examined snowflakes under a microscope tell us that every single snowflake is different. That's the wonder of God's creation, and it's true

The God We Don't Believe In

of every one of us. Each of us is different and, in some way, meant to reflect Him and fulfill a distinct part of His wonderful plan. Have you seen that poster of the poor kid with dirt on his face and ragged clothes? The caption below reads, "God don't make no junk!" Every child is a precious, priceless, and unique creation of God.

A priest who was helping in the former leper hospital in Carville, La., shared this story with a group of us. One night, he was called to administer the sacrament of the sick to a woman who was dying. She had been a very beautiful woman when she was younger, but she was all disfigured now from Hansen's disease and was dying all alone at the hospital. He anointed her and told her, because she was not at the point of death, "I'll be back tomorrow to bring you Holy Communion." The next day when he walked into the room, he was amazed at what he saw. She was all radiant with smiles.

"Why are you so happy?" he asked. "Father," she said, "a wonderful thing happened to me last night. Jesus came and spoke to me," and she quoted His words. Whether she knew it or not, the words were from the Old Testament book, "The Song of Songs," an inspired, poetic masterpiece about love—human love, but human love as a reflection of God's love. Jesus said, *"Arise my beloved, my beautiful one, and come, for see the winter has passed. The rains are over and gone. The flowers appear on the earth. The time of pruning the vines has come. And the song of the dove is heard in our land. Arise, my beloved, my beautiful one and come"* (2:10-13).

You see, you're beautiful in the sight of God because He loves you. You and I have witnessed that with some parents who have a deformed or handicapped child. If those parents love that child, the child is beautiful to them. And you're beautiful to God.

The Prophet Isaiah also says this in his 62nd chapter. *"You shall be called by a new name pronounced by the mouth of the Lord... No more shall men call you 'Forsaken'...but you shall be called 'My Delight'... For the Lord delights in you...and, as a bridegroom rejoices in his bride, so shall your God rejoice in you"* (62:4-5). Sure, God doesn't delight in everything you and I do, but He delights in **you,** the person that He created, who stands back of those acts. And He's always calling us to be fully and uniquely the persons that He created us to be.

TOUGH LOVE

There is something else about God's love: it's not a weak love, a namby-pamby love, or a sissy love. It's a strong love, a tough love. Many people have heard of the support groups called "Tough Love" which help parents to deal with rebellious and disruptive children—not violently, but firmly and decisively, out of love. This kind of tough love is a reflection of God's love for us. *"Do not disdain the discipline of the Lord or lose heart when reproved by him; for whom the Lord loves, he disciplines; he scourges every son he acknowledges"* (Heb 12:56).

Some years ago there was a documentary on TV. Though fictitious, it had an historical base. It was the story of Jane Pittman, a black woman who supposedly had lived through the days of slavery. She had witnessed and suffered so much—personally and with her family. Towards the end of the documentary, Jane Pittman—now in her nineties—is being interviewed by a TV reporter. "What do you do with your time all day?" he asks. The old lady replies, "Well, I just comes, and I sits under this tree, and I thinks and I thinks how good God is!" All the adversity, all the pain, and all the suffering had not left their bitterness but a greater closeness to and reliance upon the Lord, whose love never fails.

Illustrating this we could use an interesting and striking example of a unique initiation ceremony practiced by some of the early American Indians. When a young brave was about to enter manhood, he had to spend an entire night out in the forest unattended and unarmed. It was a fearful experience, because anything could happen. He was open to attack by an enemy tribe or a wild animal. Even the sound of a twig breaking under his feet could make his heart pound; it might be a poisonous snake. That was the test—to make it through that awful night all alone. As the hours passed so slowly, the boy could hardly wait for the darkness to end and dawn to appear. As the first rays of the early morning sun began to break through the trees, the young man looked around

The God We Don't Believe In

and noticed that—in back of a tree not far from him—**his father was there**. The father had been there all night long, his eye on his son, ready to do whatever was necessary to protect him. That's an image of God our Father. In the course of life, He allows us to pass through some very dark nights and difficult times. He never said it was going to be easy. In fact, Jesus said very clearly, *"Take up your cross and follow me,"* but He did promise that He'd be there with us every step of the way. *"Are not two sparrows sold for a small coin? Yet not one of them falls to the ground without your Father's knowledge... You are worth more than many sparrows"* (Mt 10:29-31). The disappointments and adversities of life can either make us bitter or better. It depends on what we do with them. They are occasions to retreat and be diminished or to grow and mature.

UNCONDITIONAL LOVE

God's love is also an unconditional love. We don't usually experience that kind of love in our everyday life. Most of us grow up in the "gold stars for good work" and the "I scratch your back; you scratch my back" way of life. God's love is different. We don't earn it. It's a pure gift. This was brought home to me years ago when, one night, probably at a penance service, the parable of the Prodigal Son was read. It's a parable I had heard many times, but something jumped out at me on that occasion that I had never noticed before.

It's that familiar story from Luke's Gospel, chapter 15, of a father and two sons. The rebellious son is tired of the old man, asks for his share of the inheritance, splits, and goes as far away from home as he can. He lives it up—wine, women, and gambling. Out of money, he gets a job feeding swine, which was about the lowest type of work a Jew of Jesus' day could think of, since devout Jews didn't even eat the flesh of pigs. He's so hungry that *"he longed to eat his fill of the pods on which the swine fed, but nobody gave him any"* (v.16). It's then that he decides to go back to his father—not expecting to be received any longer as a son, but just begging to be a hired hand. So he starts on the long journey

15

home.

In the parable, Jesus says that *"while he was still a long way off, his father caught sight of him"* (v 20). The son forgot the father, but the father never for a minute forgot the son. I can picture the father not only hoping and praying for his son's return, but also going out to the road day after day, longing to catch sight of the boy. Then one day, far in the distance, he sees a figure moving toward him. At first, it is small and indistinguishable, but, intuitively, the father knows, "The day has come. This is my son!"

He doesn't wait for the boy to get to the house. He can't contain himself, his love, or his joy. The father, *"filled with compassion,"* runs to his son, embraces him, and kisses him. The son says to him, *"Father, I have sinned against heaven and against you; I no longer deserve to be called your son."* Before he can complete the speech he had prepared, the father swoops him up into his arms and almost carries him into the house. He calls out to his servants, *"Quickly, bring the finest robe and put it on him; put a ring on his finger and sandals on his feet. Take the fatted calf and slaughter it. Then, let us celebrate with a feast"* (vv 20-23), and the celebration begins.

Now, this is the part that really spoke to me. It's the father's response to the elder son who was out in the field doing his daily chores while the partying was going on. As this son nears the house and hears the sound of music and dancing, he calls one of the servants and asks what's going on. When the servant tells him, he refuses, in anger, to go in. His father comes out and pleads with him. He says to his father, *"Look, all these years I served you and not once did I disobey your orders, yet you never gave me even a young goat to feast on with my friends. But when your son returns who swallowed up your property with prostitutes, for him you slaughter the fattened calf"* (vv 29-30). Now, listen carefully to the father's response: *"My son, you are here with me always; everything I have is yours.* **But now we must celebrate and rejoice,** *because your brother was dead and has come to life again; he was lost and has been found"* (vv 29-32). To paraphrase, "Son, I love you too, but **I can't help but do what I'm doing, because he's my son and that's just the way a father is."**

The God We Don't Believe In

You see, when I heard that part of the story once again, something clicked. What clicked was that God loves me. He doesn't love me because I've done everything right (and I *haven't*), and He doesn't stop loving me if I mess it all up. I can mess it up. He leaves me free. I could mess up my life now, and I could mess it up for all eternity. He won't force me to be with Him and to be a member of His household now or forever. That's my choice. But He loves me and goes on loving me and calling me to Himself until the last breath of my earthly life. He gives me that gift of His love, unconditionally. He says to you and to me, "I can't help but love you, because you're my son, you're my daughter, and that's just the way a father is. So, I'm asking you, would you just accept that free gift of my love—believe it, receive it, and let it heal and transform your life—and then live as my son or daughter?"

SONS AND DAUGHTERS

If that's the kind of Father we have, then what kind of sons and daughters should we be? The answer to that could fill volumes, but let's zero in on just three qualities. They're easy to remember; they all start with a "T": *trustful, thankful,* and *thoughtful*—thoughtful of His love and of one another. I'll share just a few ideas about each of these.

TRUSTFUL
"Fear is useless; what is needed is trust"
(Mk 5:36, NAB unrevised).

Do you really trust God? Do you entrust everything to Him? Someone has said, "I trust God with my mind, but my stomach ain't got the message yet!" I can identify with that when I get those knots or butterflies in my gut. Hopefully, as life goes along, trust will permeate our whole attitude and being more and more.

Some years ago, I heard the moving testimony of a former astronaut, Charles Duke. He told about the turning point in his life when he made the shift from just believing that God exists—*"Even the demons believe that..."* (Jas 2:19)—to entrusting himself and everything in his life to God (and the peace and joy that followed).

In that regard, I also think of something that happened to me when I was growing up that helped to teach me about trust. In elementary school, I used to cheat a lot! Some of us who were partners in crime had gotten it down to a fine art. As a result, in my final year I ended up getting a certificate for spelling, although I wasn't a good speller. After I graduated, I can still picture myself in my home in New Orleans, all alone, taking that certificate and tearing it up. I was disgusted with myself and with what I had done, and I said to myself, "I'm never going to cheat again."

That resolution was put to the test especially on one occasion in High School when a difficult science exam was scheduled. On the day before the exam, some guys in the class were able to get the prof's test, and they began to pass it around. Man, did I want to get a look at that exam! But I had said to myself, "I'm not going to cheat again," so I decided to stick to it. The next day, we all shuffled into the classroom and sat down. The prof came in and gave out the test—but it was not the test that had been passed around! The guys who had relied on it were in big trouble, but, since I had studied and tried to prepare, I was able to pass.

It taught me that God doesn't sleep. You and I can cut corners. We can lie and cheat, wheel and deal, and do all kinds of wrongful things to solve our problems. God sees it all. Your life and my life are in His hands. Everything we have comes from Him. We need to use it all the way He wants us to use it. In one moment, He could take it all away. In one moment, He can give us everything we need. He simply asks that we trust Him—entrust it **all** to Him— and seek to do His will in everything.

The night before Jesus died, He prayed a simple prayer—profoundly simple and profoundly difficult at the same time, *"...not my will, but yours be done"* (Lk 22:42). Out of that surrender came the resurrection and the redemption of the world. If you and I could only pray that prayer every day from the heart! When we say the Our Father, really mean, "Thy will be done." Would that we could pray, "God I want to do your will. Today in all the difficult situations I'm facing, I want to do what you want me to do. I'm not going to worry about how it's going to work out, or what they're going to think of me, or what the consequences are going to be. I just want to do what you want me to do. Give me the strength to do that, for, of myself, I can't." Then, be at peace and trust Him—surrendering all to Him.

Jesus said, *"Do not worry...but seek first the kingdom [of God] and his righteousness, and all these things will be given you besides"* (Mt 6:30-33). There's that beautiful spiritual based on those other words of Jesus when He spoke about God our Father watching over the tiniest sparrow.

> "I sing because I'm happy.
> I sing because I'm free.
> His eye is on the sparrow,
> And I know he watches me."

Oh yes, He does—every one of us. As life has gone along, it has been a deeply moving and remarkable thing to experience the providential hand of God at work when I do manage to trust Him and surrender to His will.

How much God desires that trust was confirmed by the many apparitions of Our Lord to Saint Faustina of Poland. After a vision in February of 1931, Our Lord asked Faustina to have the image she had seen painted, reproduced, and circulated everywhere. Below His image, He wanted the words, *"Jesus, I trust in You."* I try to begin every day with these words, not because I trust Him that much, but because I know that I don't and pray that trust will grow.

THANKFUL
"In all circumstances give thanks..." (Thes 16-18).

Secondly, thank Him. Once I devoted an entire private retreat at Madonna House in Canada to the theme of thanksgiving. What I did was to go back over my whole life and thank God for everything: my parents, my family and friends, the schools I went to, all the experiences I'd had—both happy and unhappy, the ups and the downs, **everything**—even what I disliked most about myself. When the retreat was over, I was filled to the brim with thanksgiving. I can still picture myself that morning on the bus heading down to Toronto. Looking out of the window, I was saying, "Thank you God for the sky. Thank you for the telephone poles. Thank you for the road. Thank you for the bus. Thank you for the driver. Thank you for everything." That's the way to go through life—not taking anything for granted. If you're able to move one hand, if you're able to say one word, if you have one piece of bread on the table, it's all a gift of God.

One of the most brilliant professors that I ever had in the seminary was Fr. Joe Buckley, S.M. One day they found Joe on the floor of his room. He had had a stroke. From that day, he was no longer able to speak one coherent sentence, and yet, his mind was apparently still clear. At least one side of his body was paralyzed. That could happen to any one of us. If we have anything, if we're able to do anything—to think, to speak, to move—it's all a gift of God. Thank Him. Thank Him for everything. Go through life thanking Him. Someone has said, "It must be tough to be an atheist, because, when you're happy, you don't know whom to thank." But we **know** whom to thank, and we can say, "Thank you, Lord." Someone else has said, "You can't be grateful and unhappy at the same time." So, cultivate an attitude of gratitude!

On that retreat, I learned something special which I hadn't really understood before. **I realized the value of thanking God—not just for the obviously easy and pleasing things of life, but for the difficult and painful ones as well.** I had brought along with me a book by Merlin Carothers entitled *Power in Praise*. Through true-life stories, he illustrates how thanking God for the contradictions of life and for the things that don't go our way can have a profound effect for good—not only on those who give thanks, but also on the situations themselves. Let me share with you just one of his examples.

There was a couple whose daughter had been declared hopelessly insane and placed in a mental institution. They had prayed and asked God to heal their daughter, but there was no change in her condition. Then one day, they went to a talk by Carothers, who told his listeners to thank God for everything in their lives—even the difficulties, pains, and contradictions.

The God We Don't Believe In

When they went home, they were upset. "We don't understand," they said. "We can thank God for many things, but we can't thank God for a daughter who's in a mental institution and has been declared hopelessly insane. **That's** insane!" As they discussed this with each other on and on and time passed, the man finally said to his wife, "Honey, you know this isn't helping our daughter. Why don't we try to do what the man said?"

Reluctantly at first, but then from their hearts, they took the matter into prayer. The husband led the prayer and said something like this: "Father, we don't understand about our daughter, but we do believe that you love her, even a thousand times more than we do. So today, we're going to say something we've never said before. Thank you for our daughter. Thank you for her just as she is. Thank you that, up to now, the doctors have not found a way to help her. You know how much we want her to get well, but we trust you and entrust her to you. We believe there must be something good you want to do or teach through this mysterious illness, so we just put her in your hands and say thank you." The longer they prayed, the more a new peace came into their hearts, a conviction that their daughter was truly in the hands of a loving God and Father.

The next morning, the telephone in their house rang. It was the hospital psychiatrist. They couldn't believe what they were hearing, but the voice on the other end of the line was saying, "We don't know what's happened, but there's been a remarkable change in your daughter. I suggest you come and see her." Two weeks later, the girl was released from the hospital. A year later, the girl's brother met Carothers at another talk and told him she was perfectly well, happily married, about to have a baby, and the "happiest girl in the world."

Now, I'm not proposing that every time you thank God, it's going to happen just that way. What I do propose is that **thanking God for life's troubles is a profound act of trust, and that trust brings peace.** Also, God could be waiting for you to make that act of trust and surrender before He goes on to do something different in your life.

As I look back over my life, I can see the hand of God in the difficult times, bringing me closer to Him **more** than in the easy times. I can identify with something about God's ways that I picked up from the testimony of the famous preacher and healer, Kathryn Kulman. She said that, as she looked back over her life, both the mountain tops and the valleys, she could see the hand of God especially in the valleys.

I'm learning to thank Him in the valleys—big or little—like when my old car would break down far from home in out-of-the-way places. It not only changed my attitude toward the situation and lifted my spirit, but, amazingly, at times help would come from out of the blue! When the old car was stolen, some friends commented that that too was an act of God, forcing me to get a new one.

Let me tell you one experience with the new one. Some years ago, I was invited to conduct a mission revival in a small town in southwest Louisiana. On Sunday evening after I had introduced the mission at all the Masses, the pastor asked me to lead the prayers at a wake service for one of his parishioners, since he had to go away for something. After leaving the funeral home and heading back to the rectory, I got lost and ended up on the highway out of town. Realizing I had gone too far, I turned onto a side road and ended up in a ditch. If you've ever had the experience, you know the awful sound and feeling of wheels turning but going nowhere. There were houses around, but it was late. Lights were out. Dogs were barking. I decided to close up the car, walk back to the highway, and hunt for help. Maybe I'd get to a phone and find someone still at the funeral home. Before I started back to the highway, I remembered **to thank God for the situation I was in**. Then the thought came, "Don't go back to the highway, but go to the nearest house. They're asleep, but go anyway." As I hesitantly approached the door of the house, out of the corner of my eye I spotted a truck in the driveway, but didn't pay it much attention. When I rang the bell, a man came to the door, listened to my story, and, in a few minutes, had me out of the ditch and on my way. He had a wrecker in the driveway! Thank God even for troubles.

It's good to remember that the word Eucharist is derived from a Greek word which means *thanksgiving*. Every time we go to

Mass, we're joining in the greatest act of communal and public thanksgiving. It's the way Jesus Himself gave us the night before He died—replacing and fulfilling the Jewish Passover sacrifice and supper—to thank our Father for everything.

THOUGHTFUL
"Remain in my love" (Jn 15:9).

Finally, be thoughtful. What good does it do to read all these pious thoughts, say, "That was nice," but then get on with the every-day grind and just forget all about it? We're called to live and move in the presence of God every day. Our Lord says, *"As the Father loves me, so I also love you.* **Remain** *in my love. If you keep my commandments, you will remain in my love, just as I have kept my Father's commandments and* **remain in his love***"* (Jn 15:9-10). The challenge is to be ever more conscious of and surrendered to God's love in our daily lives—sharing it with everyone. St. John says, *"Beloved, if God so loved us, we must also love one another"* (1 Jn 4:11).

Mother Theresa of Calcutta used to say that there are two things that everybody in the world is hunting for. Whether we live in Calcutta, New York, or New Orleans, and whatever our life's circumstances, we're all searching for the same two basic things—**to love and to be loved.** You don't have to go around the world to find them. You don't have to knock yourself out. Just stop right now and open the door of your heart. **Accept the mystery that God loves you, respond in love by surrendering to His will, and share His love with others.**

Love is our calling. It's our life, our joy. This is not just religion; it's good psychology as well. We're living fully only when we're loving fully and letting ourselves be loved. The problem for many of us is that we're only half alive! The other half is preoccupied with the past or future, and we're missing the **present moment of life and love.**

So many of us go through our daily lives dragging with us sad thoughts and memories of the past. We're preoccupied with the things that we've done wrong, the opportunities we missed, and the people we neglected or hurt. We keep toting that along like a sack on our back.

What can we do about it all? We can let it go! We don't have to keep dragging it with us. It's unnecessary. **Everything that you and I have ever done wrong can be brought to Jesus and laid down at the foot of His cross.** He died on that cross so that our sins could be forgiven.

Ask Him, by His blood shed for you, to do just that. Tell Him you're sorry for all the sins of your life, especially out of love for Him who loves you so much. Open your heart, like a door, and invite Him in to lead, guide, and use you from now on. If you're Catholic, also take another step and bring all these troubling things to the Sacrament of Reconciliation. This sacrament is the earthly visible sign and instrument of His forgiveness and the forgiveness of His Church. Then, leave it there and go away, free and new. Let go of that guilt. It's no joy to God and certainly no help for you to hold on to it once you've been forgiven. *"Though your sins be as scarlet, I will make them white as wool"* (Is 1:18).

What about the people who have injured you? Is there any one of us who has never been hurt by someone else? All of us have been injured many many times, and, we've done our share of injuring. What do we do about all that? Do we go through life just letting hurt be added to hurt until it becomes a huge open wound that never heals? That doesn't have to be. It's not God's will for us. If He can forgive us—if He, the almighty and infinitely good God, whom you and I have offended, can forgive us—then you and I can forgive one another.

Forgiveness is a decision, not a feeling. To forgive is not to whitewash the wrong or to say wrong is right. It's a willingness to let go of the poison, bitterness, hatred, revenge, and all the ill feelings that are lodged within us because of the wrong—real or imagined. It's a healthy and godly decision in line with the old dictum: to err is human; to forgive is divine.

I recall a statement I read years ago from Daddy King, the erudite father of the famed civil rights leader, Martin Luther King. There were those who wondered about his attitude after his son was assassinated and then later, his own dear wife murdered. Clearly (and in dialect for emphasis), he stated, "I ain't mad at nobody." Like his son, he continued to believe that hatred would not be overcome by more hatred—but only by forgiveness and love.

I also remember an interview for radio I once had with the mother of a little child who had been killed. The perpetrator was in Parchman Prison in Mississippi. Forgiveness proved to be a great struggle for her, but, as a conscientious Catholic Christian, she tried. God gave her the grace especially on a spiritual retreat. As time passed and she continued to pray, she received a further inspiration to go and see the man and let him know she had forgiven him. Arrangements for the visit required time and effort (contacting the prison authorities, the chaplain, the prisoner himself to make sure he was willing to meet, etc.). Finally the day came, and she arrived at Parchman Prison. The man was brought in, but he was too ashamed even to look at her.

"It's taken a lot out of me to come here today," she said, "and for what I have to say, I want you to look at me." When he did, she continued, "I want you to know that I forgive you."

During his entire imprisonment, the man had expressed no emotion about what he had done—but after those words, he broke down and began to cry. It was the beginning of a whole new life for him.

Actually, the mother—supported by her husband—went to court at the time of his trial to plead that his life be spared. Probably, without giving it the name, she was practicing the spirit of what we now call "**restorative justice**." She recognized the man's need to repair the injustice he had done and was not asking otherwise. *Rather than just take revenge and destroy another life, however, she chose to help restore two lives—his and hers.*

All you and I need to do is to go to Jesus and say, "Jesus, I open my heart to you. I have trouble forgiving, but I want to. You know my heart and my hurts. You died for me and for all who have injured me. Forgive and heal me with your love. *Let me be an instrument of your forgiveness and love to others.* You take over. Let it be you who forgives in and through me. Then it will be your great forgiveness and love and not just my own."

Once you make the decision to forgive, keep it alive by often—even daily—including the forgiven in your prayers. Every time the old negative feeling wells up inside and you pray, practicing forgiveness, you're doing a holy, meritorious thing. Doing that day after day, little by little, your heart may be healed. In addition to that, you could often practice what is called the "healing of memories" either privately or with another's prayerful help. A common way of fostering such healing is by inviting Jesus into the hurtful memory and, if possible, picturing Him (and maybe Mary, too) present with you at the time it happened. Then, let them do or say whatever they choose in that circumstance. An ideal time for this would be after Holy Communion. Remarkable healings, or at least the beginning of healings, have taken place in this way.

Then, **forgive yourself.** Some of us can ask God's forgiveness, and we can forgive others, but we never forgive ourselves. Why not? If God forgives you, and you forgive others, why not forgive yourself? *"Love your neighbor as yourself,"* He told us (Mt 22:38), and, if you ask, He'll give the grace for that as well.

There may be a hidden pride in self-unforgiveness. Perhaps we tell ourselves, "I'm a good person. How could I have ever done such a thing?" Instead, we could humbly say, "I did it, Lord, and without your grace, I could do worse. Whatever responsibility was mine, help me accept it as You alone know it. Forgive me and give me the grace to forgive myself."

What about the future? When we let the past go, we might still be troubled about what lies ahead. There could be an onslaught of concerns. Suppose I get cancer or lose my job? Suppose my husband or wife, son or daughter, parent or friend becomes estranged from me? Suppose the project I'm working on doesn't pan out? Suppose, suppose, suppose.

Sure, there are seemingly endless possibilities, but it's all in God's hands. "I don't know what the future holds," someone has said, "but I know who holds the future." The same God who watched over you yesterday and the day before will be there tomorrow and the day after. You're His son or daughter. If He feeds the birds of the air and clothes the flowers of the field, if He watches over the tiniest sparrow, certainly He'll watch over you, who *"are worth more than many sparrows"* (Mt 10:31). *"Can any of you by worry-*

ing add a single moment to your life span? ... Do not worry about tomorrow; tomorrow will take care of itself" (Mt 6:27 & 34).

So, take the burden of the past and bring it all to Jesus, accepting His forgiveness, forgiving others, and forgiving yourself. Entrust the future to the Father's loving care. Then, live life fully, one day at a time—each hour, each moment. The truth is that the **only real life is this one present moment**. The past is gone; the future isn't here. To miss the moment, the "now," is to miss life and to miss God. *"Behold, **now** is a very acceptable time; behold, **now** is the day of salvation"* (2 Cor 6:2). **The great truth of our faith, revealed to us by Jesus and standing back of all the others, is that God our Father is at work at every moment, offering you the amazing gift of His love and inviting you to respond and grow in love for Him and everyone.**

***

A prayer for healing of hurtful memories from conception through adulthood can be found in the appendix.

Love's the Message that I Heard

CHAPTER 2

Who Is Jesus Christ?
The difference between knowing about and knowing

ONE SOLITARY LIFE

He was born in an obscure village, the child of a peasant woman. He grew up in still another village, where he worked in a carpenter shop until he was thirty. Then for three years, he was an itinerant preacher. He never wrote a book. He never held an office. He never had a family or owned a house. He didn't go to college. He never visited a big city. He never traveled two hundred miles from the place he was born.

He did none of the things one usually associates with greatness. He had no credentials but himself. He was only thirty-three when the tide of public opinion turned against him. His friends ran away. He was turned over to his enemies and went through the mockery of a trial. He was nailed to a cross between two thieves. While he was dying, his executioners gambled for his clothing, the only property he had on earth. When he was dead, he was laid in a borrowed grave through the pity of a friend.

Nineteen centuries have come and gone, and today he is the central figure of the human race and the leader of mankind's progress. All the armies that ever marched, all the navies that ever sailed, all the parliaments that ever sat, all the kings that ever reigned, put together, have not affected the life of man on this earth as much as that ONE SOLITARY LIFE.

(Anonymous)

All of human history, from the beginning of time to this day, is divided by the coming of Jesus Christ. Whenever we date a document, a letter, or anything—whether we're people of faith or not—we write 2002, 2005, or 2025, etc. What does it mean except that there have been that many years since the birth of Christ? All the time before Him is called B.C.—Before Christ, and all the time after Him, A.D.—in Latin, Anno Domini, literally "in the year of the Lord." Of course, today there are those who are trying to change all that and get Christ out of the picture wherever they can. Nevertheless, His life remains the central event of history.

Who is Jesus Christ? He is also the centerpiece of the most widely circulated book in the world and the first book of modern-day printing—the Bible. It's a book about Jesus. The Old Testament leads up to Him, preparing the way, foreshadowing, and foretelling Him. The New Testament is all about Him, His life, His works, His teachings, and His Church. From that book, He emerges as the greatest miracle worker and teacher of righteousness, by word and example, that the world has ever known.

All that we have thus far said about Jesus could be said even by people without faith. Who, then, is Jesus for people of faith?

MESSIAH

Jesus asked His apostles, "*Who do you say that I am?*" and Peter answered, "*You are the Messiah, the Son of the living God.*" "*Flesh and blood has not revealed this to you*," Jesus said, "*but my heavenly Father*" (Mt 16:15-17). Only by the gift of faith can any of us make this affirmation—a gift to ask God to give if you don't have it and to strengthen if you do. The Scriptures, tradition, and all believing Christians witness, first of all, to the great truth that He is the Messiah. What does that mean?

For two thousand years, beginning with Abraham, God formed a people. He prepared them for the time in history when Jesus Christ would come. He raised up patriarchs and prophets who called these Israelites back to God when they wandered away, taught them His way and His will, and, from time to time, told them about a special emissary of God, a Messiah who was to come. Among other things, they foretold that He would be born of a virgin and of the ancestry of King David and would be called *"The Lord our justice"* (Jer 23:56) and *"Immanuel"*—a name meaning *"With us is God"* (Is 7:14). They prophesied that Bethlehem would be His place of origin (Mi 5:14). They not only predicted His unparalleled healing and teaching ministry but also that He would be rejected, put to death, and rise again. (e.g. Ps 16 & 22; Is 8:23 to 9:6; and Is 40-55, the Suffering Servant songs.)

In the Old Testament, we find at least thirty prophecies (perhaps even three hundred) that were fulfilled in Jesus. We hear these proclaimed in the Scriptures at Mass, especially during Advent and Lent. Actually, if we look into it deeply enough, **all** of the events of the Old Testament were a foreshadowing of and preparation for what was going to happen through Jesus and His Church.

Listen to the words of one of those old, immortal, faith filled Christmas Carols, "O Little Town of Bethlehem":

In your dark streets shineth the everlasting light.
The hopes and fears of all the years
Are met in thee tonight.

In Him can be fulfilled the deepest hopes and dreams of every human heart, and all our fears can be overcome. He is the Messiah, the long expected One. With Martha, Christians testify *"Yes, Lord. I have come to believe that you are the Messiah, the Son of God, the one who is coming into the world"* (Jn 11:27).

SAVIOR

He is also Savior. The angel instructed Joseph, *"...you are to name him Jesus, because he will save his people from their sins"* (Mt 1:21). We Catholics are reminded of that truth every time we look at a crucifix or go to Mass. **His death was more than just another horrible execution. It was a sacrifice He freely offered for the salvation of the world.** As Isaiah the prophet had foretold, *"He was pierced for our offenses, crushed for our sins; upon him was the chastisement that makes us whole, by his stripes we were* *healed*" (Is 53:5). Only through Him has heaven been opened again, and only through Him do we receive the grace to get there.

OUR LORD AND OUR GOD

With Thomas the Apostle, we also testify that He is *"My Lord and my God!"* (Jn 20:28). If Jesus Christ was not—is not—our Lord and God, then He was the greatest imposter, prideful person, or fool who ever lived. Hardly anyone claims that about Jesus, yet He *acted as God, spoke as God*, and *said He was God*.

He acted as God. By His own power and word of command, He stilled the storm on the sea (Mk 4:35-41, Lk 8:22-25) and changed water into wine (Jn 2:1-11). He miraculously multiplied loaves of bread and fish (Mt 15:32-38) and healed the sick (Mk 2:1-12). He expelled demons (Mk 1:21-28) and raised the dead (Lk 7:11-17), just to mention some of His miracles. He also forgave sins, which the Jews of His day recognized as something only God could do, accusing Jesus of blasphemy (Mt 9:3, Mk 2:7, Lk 5:21). He did all the above in His own name and by His own power. When His followers perform miracles or His Church forgives sins, it's done *in His name and by His power*.

He spoke as God with definitive *"authority and not as the scribes"* (Mt 7:29). He said, *"Whoever loves father or mother more than me is not worthy of me, and whoever loves son or daughter more than me is not worthy of me"* (Mt 10:37). He claimed that, at the final judgment, people of all nations would be assembled before Him, *"the king,"* and that the judgment would be *"Whatever you did* (or neglected to do) *for one of these least brothers of mine,* ***you did for me***" (Mt 25:31-46). Only God could say such things.

He said He was God. *"The Father and I are one"* (Jn 10:30), and *"Amen, amen I say to you, before Abraham came to be, I am"* (Jn 8:58), He asserted, pointing to His oneness of nature and eternal existence with the Father. He called Himself God's unique, divine Son, sharing life and knowledge with His Father as no one else. *"No one knows who the Son is except the Father, and who the Father is except the Son and anyone to whom the Son wishes to reveal him"* (Lk 10:22b). He said, *"All power in heaven and on* *earth has been given to me"* and instructed His Church to baptize *"in the name* (not the names) *of the Father, and of the Son, and of the Holy Spirit,"* proclaiming one God and three distinct but equally divine persons (Mt 28:18-19).

St. Paul, who came later but was instructed by Jesus Himself and the apostles, understood the meaning of Christ and His Gospel and proclaims His divinity. In his letter to the Colossians Paul says, *"For in him were created all things in heaven and on earth...all things were created through him and for him"* (1:16) and *"For in Him dwells the whole fullness of the deity bodily"* (2:9). In the prologue of his Gospel, John says, *"In the beginning was the Word, and the Word was with God, and the Word was God...and the Word became flesh and made his dwelling among us..."* (Jn 1:1 & 14). Jesus is God in the flesh—completely human, completely divine, in the unity of one person, Jesus Christ, Son of God.

WHO IS JESUS FOR YOU?

Now, that's who Jesus is—the Messiah, the Savior, and the divine Son of God. But who is Jesus for you? You might go through your entire life saying you believe all this, yet it could still have little or no effect on your daily life and conduct. The Bible says even the devils *"believe...and tremble"* (Jas 2:19). The mere belief hasn't changed their lives for the better.

Some years ago on television, there would appear from time to time a brief segment that featured a Dallas Cowboy football game. In it, the Cowboys make a beautiful catch in the end-zone. Then the camera shifts to the sidelines and focuses on the coach, Tom Landry. The announcer says, "Tom Landry—probably one of the greatest coaches of our day. You would certainly think *football* is the great passion of his life." Then, the scene changes and you see Tom Landry in his home. He says, "You know the most important thing in my life? It's my relationship with Our Lord, Jesus Christ."

What's the most important thing in your life? Can you say that simple thing Tom Landry said? When I look back on my own life, even some of my life as a priest, I don't think I would have said that. I would have said that Jesus Christ was the most important one in my life, but I don't think I would have talked about my *relationship* with Him. I knew about Jesus. I had studied about Jesus. I could tell other people about Jesus, but I didn't know Jesus in a deep personal way. I didn't know Him the way that a friend knows a friend, or the way a good husband and wife are meant to know and grow in knowledge and love and sharing with one another. I could have, and many of my fellow Catholics did, but I didn't know Jesus in that way.

As a young priest, I threw myself into the thick of parish ministry and became busy with many things. I was working with youth, meeting regularly with groups of married couples in the exciting new Christian Family Movement, and I was concerned and active with issues of social and interracial justice and peace, especially in the life of the Church.

As the years went along however, I noticed that, deep down in my own heart, there was a frequent restlessness, a hunger, and a lack of peace. I went through a long time of spiritual direction and searching to try to find out what was wrong or what was missing. I also sought professional help. For a while, I thought that maybe I had missed my vocation and shouldn't be a priest. This soul-searching helped me get in touch with some of my own unrealistic expectations, fears, and neurotic compulsions. Most of all, it led me to understand that the main thing that was missing was my **personal relationship with Jesus Christ.**

Every human being (knowingly or unknowingly) longs for personal relationships. We seek them in friendships and in marriage, but behind it all is the desire (known or unknown) for the ultimate relationship with God in Jesus Christ. After all his searching, Augustine cried out, "Our hearts are made for you, O God, and they are restless until they rest in You." Jesus said, *"I am the bread of life. Whoever comes to me will never hunger, and whoever believes in me will never thirst"* (Jn 6:35). I discovered that there was a hunger in my heart that He alone could fill and a thirst inside me that He alone, the source of *"living water"* (Jn 4:10), could quench.

I was an assistant in a downtown parish. I had my duties, but, in the midst of them, I made a commitment to stop being "too busy," to cut out some unnecessary things, and, for a year, to seek one thing above all—to deepen my relationship with Him.

The first thing I knew I had to do to make that possible was to **take more time each day to pray**. What's missing in so many relationships and in so many marriages is *communication*—taking time for it and being honest in it. I realized then that I needed more honest communication with the Lord. I needed to open up, lay out my whole life before Him, and allow Him to do in me or say to me all that He wanted.

As I began to do that, to take a good chunk of time each day (at least an hour) especially in the presence of our Lord in the Blessed Sacrament, I found it tough—one of the toughest things I had ever decided to do. Time and time again, I didn't want to be there. I wanted to run. I could think of all the other things that I thought I had to do or that I wanted to do, but, as I went back day after day, He convinced me that the main thing that I had to do—that I needed to do—was pray. (I was learning that "when you're too busy to pray, you're too busy!") What I experienced as I daily "sweated it out" in His presence was that I was sweating out the things that were barriers between me and Him.

I think about something that I read years ago in an introduction to a book on prayer by Thomas Merton. The introduction says that prayer is something like the old theater houses where there used to be three curtains. One curtain would go up, then the second, and finally the third; then, you were face to face with the players. Prayer is something like that. As we go back to pray day after day in the course of our lives, little by little—almost imperceptibly—the barriers and defenses between us and the Lord begin to come down, and we're more and more face to face with Him.

It was that kind of thing that I experienced as I returned to prayer again and again. I realized that what I was sweating out were a lot of things that I had not faced before, that I didn't even know about: my pride, self-centeredness, laziness, self-indulgence, and so on down the line. He was breaking through; walls were coming down.

The second thing I did that year was to **read the Bible in a new way**. Everyone who prepares for the priesthood studies the

Scriptures deeply, and I had studied them. It was also a required part of our seminary rule that we would take at least fifteen minutes every day to read the Bible. I did that, but I did it mechanically. I did it because I had to do it; however, that year of my life, ten years after ordination, I did it because I wanted to do it—because I was hungry for God. Jerome, a saint of the Catholic Church, lived three hundred years after Christ and spent much of his life poring over the Scriptures and translating them to make them available to the people of his day. St. Jerome said, "Ignorance of the Scriptures is ignorance of Jesus." I didn't want to be ignorant of Him.

As I took more time each day to read the Bible, there were sections that I found uninteresting and passages that seemed to have little meaning for my life, but as I continued to read, something began to happen. Like streetlights coming on in the dark, the words of Scripture began to light up for me, and I realized that what I was reading was not just the story of something that had happened a long time ago. Through the words and events of Scripture, God was speaking to me now; God was touching my life! I began to see the relationship between what I was reading and what was happening around me and within me, and I started to write down these insights.

The third thing I did (at least for that year) was to **practice a little more self-discipline** (a part of *disciple*ship), especially concerning food. I hail from an old New Orleans restaurant family where eating together was a daily routine and food preparation an art. Even to make some small sacrifices in that regard was a big thing for me! What I experienced was what the Scriptures, tradition, and the Church tell us. There is an intimate connection between fasting (even eating healthfully and moderately), or whatever type of self-denial or self-discipline we accept, and opening our hearts to God. It's something that none of us like, but all of us need in our lifetime walk with the Lord—learning to say "no" to ourselves (sometimes even in legitimate things), so we can more readily say "yes" to God.

When that year was over, I experienced a new peace in my life. When I lose it now, I know where to find it. I find it in Him who is the *"Prince of Peace"* (Is 9:5), the source of our peace.

There was a new relationship with Him—**as my brother and friend, my Savior, and the Lord of my life.** I also realized that what I had begun was a journey—not for a day, a month, or a year—but for a lifetime. As the song from the musical *Godspell* puts it: "To see thee more clearly, love thee more dearly, and follow thee more nearly day by day." I knew that, if God gives me one more day, it was more important than anything else that I use it for that.

JESUS AT THE CENTER

I also realized—better than I had ever realized before—the simple truth that **the center of everything that I was doing as a priest and everything we do as Catholic Christians is Our Lord Jesus Christ.** The story is told about the visitor to New York who asked the cab driver on a Sunday morning to take him to the Church of Christ. The Irish cabbie drove into the heart of Manhattan and deposited the man at the steps of St. Patrick's Cathedral. "Hey," the passenger objected, "this is not the Church of Christ!" "Buddy," the cabbie responded, "if he ain't here, he ain't in town."

Walk into the average Catholic church and what things immediately catch your eye? Usually they are front and center: the *crucifix*, that powerful image of Jesus Christ, Savior of the world; the *altar* on which is carried out His command *"do this in memory of me"* (Lk 22:19); the *pulpit* from which His word is proclaimed and preached; and close by, the *tabernacle* containing Him, *"the bread of life...the bread that comes down from heaven..."* (Jn 6:48-49).

Yes, the typical Catholic church building is centered around Jesus Christ, but more important, this is true of the world-wide Catholic Church. He's her center, focus, and purpose—of every sacrament and teaching, of every law and devotion.

Every sacrament of the Church is a meeting with Jesus under a sacred sign. Jesus isn't walking around among us the same way He walked among the people of Galilee or Palestine, but, because we're human beings, we want to be able to *see* and *touch* and *hear* something; we want to *contact* God in a down-to-earth, *concrete* way. God knows that we want this; He knows that in a certain sense we even need it. That's the reason (or at least one of the reasons) for the Incarnation—Jesus Christ, God in the flesh. That's the reason for the Church and the sacraments—those sacred signs of His presence, His working among us.

Every one of those seven sacraments is an encounter with Jesus Christ. He's what they're all about. In Baptism, it's Jesus who immerses us in His death and resurrection and joins us to His body, the Church. In Reconciliation, He's the one who again reconciles us to the Father and to one another through His Church. In the Anointing of the Sick, He's the one whose healing power is going out. He's the one imparting the gift of the Holy Spirit to those confirmed, ordained to the ministry, or joined together in marriage. Especially in the sacrament of sacraments, the Holy Eucharist, He's the one calling us over and over again to unite ourselves to His eternal surrender to the Father and feeding us with His own Body and Blood. The sacraments are meetings with Him and, in the community of His Church, celebrations of Jesus Christ—His life, His work, and His ministry.

Every teaching of the Church is connected with Our Blessed Lord. Whether it's about eternal life that He opened up to us, about grace and salvation which come from Him, about the Church, which is His body, or about how to live in this world following Him—all of it is centered in Jesus Christ, Our Lord.

All law and authority in the Church is also ultimately centered in Him. Besides divine law (e.g. respect for life), why do we have certain Church laws (such as Sunday Mass) and authority anyway? Every family, every organization, every group of people that wants to stay together and be committed to some work needs leadership, legitimate authority, and some rules and regulations to hold them together. Our Catholic family spread out over the earth is no exception, but this leadership, this authority, and these rules are there for a purpose. *They're there to hold us together with one another around Our Lord Jesus Christ, our Head, so that together we might continue His mission.*

Every devotion in the Church, no matter what, **is related to Jesus**. For example, take the devotion to the saints. Why do we honor the saints and ask their intercession? We honor them for a simple reason. *They are examples of what it means to follow Jesus, and they help us to do the same.* They were men, women, and young people like us. They were black and white, yellow and red. They lived in all manner of circumstances, in diverse cultures, and in many different parts of the world. They put up with all the troubles and difficulties—and usually much more—that you and I put up with. They experienced the onslaught of temptation, and, if and when they fell along the way, they repented and turned back to Him. Through it all, Jesus Christ became for them the Lord and center of their lives, and *they hung on to Him to their dying breath*, proclaiming Him to others. The Church honors them in order to say to us, "Following Jesus is for us real live human beings of today. They did it, and you can do it. They're that mighty company of *'witnesses'* (Heb 12:1-2) pulling for you, praying for you, and calling out, "Hang in there. We made it, and you can make it too!"

The official prayers of the Church, as we notice at Mass, usually end with the phrase, "...through Jesus Christ, our Lord," recognizing Him as the *"one mediator between God and the human race"* (1 Tim 2:5). We can use all the help we can get, and the saints are part of our spiritual family. Just like we can and should pray for one another all along the way in this life, the saints in heaven don't forget us when they get to "the other shore" but can still be with us in a communion of love and prayer. The ancient Apostles Creed recited by Christians of different denominations professes faith in "the communion of saints." A consistent practice of the Church from the earliest times testifies to this, with evidence even in catacomb inscriptions. The last book of the Bible also depicts the saints offering *"the prayers of the holy ones"* (Rev 5:8) like incense before God's throne.

As you read the lives of the saints, what do you notice? Typically, **they were men and women who had a deep, personal relationship with Our Lord Jesus Christ**. Their hearts were on fire with love for Him. Take a man like Ignatius of Loyola. The religious community he founded was originally called *The Company of Jesus* (in line with his military background). Alphonsus Ligouri, with his brilliant mind, composed that prayer I learned as a child at the regular devotions of the Stations of the Cross:

> I love You Jesus, my love. I love You more than myself. I repent with my whole heart for having offended You. Never permit me to separate myself from You again. Grant that I may love You always, and then do with me what is Your will.

A woman like Margaret Mary, to whom Our Lord appeared with His heart ablaze with love, spent her life proclaiming the mystery of Jesus' personal love for each of us. Therese, called "the little flower of Jesus," died at the young age of twenty-four. Under obedience, she wrote her autobiography, *The Story of a Soul*. Every page burns with love for Our Lord. One after the other, these men and women had a deep personal love for Jesus and, as a result, an ever-growing love for all their sisters and brothers. At the top of the list is the one who had the closest relationship of all to Our Lord—Mary, His Mother.

Sometimes when we hear about the saints, we think, "Well, that was okay for them, but it's not for me." The Church honors them in order to say their personal love for Jesus is a model for us all. We're all called to genuine holiness, as the Second Vatican Council reminds us. We're all called to grow every day in knowing, loving, and serving Our Lord, Jesus Christ. That's our goal, and everything we do in the Church is ultimately meant to foster it.

What I'm saying is this: sometimes we're like people who miss the forest for the trees. The trees are the sacraments, the teachings, the laws, and the devotions. They're beautiful; they're needed. Appreciate them. Don't neglect them. They're God's gift and plan for you. They're there for a purpose. **They are there to lead us to an ever-deepening relationship with Our Lord Jesus Christ at the center**. They're there that we might grow in knowing Him, loving Him, and surrendering ourselves to Him so that He might become more and more the Lord of our lives and use us to continue His mission. He's the forest. They're the trees. To miss Him would be to miss the point of it all.

Let me pause here. The truth is so simple: Jesus is the center of everything in the Church, but maybe we take it for granted and don't say it enough. Maybe some of us priests and teachers don't personally have enough of a relationship with Him (as I didn't) to foster it sufficiently in others. For this, I beg forgiveness. He's at the center of what we're all about. He's what the Church has been all about for 2000 years. *For the times any of us members of that Church have obscured that truth, bungled it, misrepresented it—please forgive us.* As the bishops of the world expressed it at the beginning of the 2nd Vatican Council, pray that "We as pastors devote all our energies and thoughts to the renewal of ourselves and the flocks committed to us so that there may radiate before all men the lovable features of Jesus Christ…" (Message to Humanity, Oct. 20, 1962).

MY BROTHER, FRIEND, AND BRIDEGROOM
"I have called you friends…" (Jn 15:18b).

What does it mean to have a personal relationship with Him? In other words, who is Jesus for you? First of all, He's our brother and our friend. *"No one has greater love than this, to lay down one's life for one's friends. You are my friends if you do what I command you"* (Jn 15:13-14). He's even called *"the bridegroom"* (Jn 3:29) The closest human relationship is between a man and a woman in marriage. Even that is only an image or reflection of the relationship Jesus wants to have with His bride, the Church—with each one of us (Eph 5:21-32). When God created man and woman, He had that in mind. It's an earthly image of a divine reality—the eternal love and life-giving union of Father, Son, and Holy Spirit—and in time of Christ and His Church.

The popular 60's song, "Bridge Over Troubled Water," by Paul Simon and Art Garfunkle, has these lyrics:

When you're weary, feeling small,
When tears are in your eyes, I'll dry them all. I'm on your side,
O, when times get rough and friends just can't be found.
Like a bridge over troubled water, I will lay me down.

Love's the Message that I Heard

> When you're down and out, when you're on the streets,
> When evening falls so hard, I'll comfort you
> I'll take your part, when darkness comes and pain is all around
> Like a bridge over troubled water, I will lay me down.
>
> Sail on, silver girl, sail on by. Your time has come to shine;
> All your dreams are on their way. See how they shine.
> And if you need a friend, I'm sailing right behind.
> Like a bridge over troubled water, I will ease your mind.

This song expresses what we all long for in a friendship. It's the kind of friend we want to have, and it's the kind of friend we want to be; however, all of us fall short of that ideal. Only Jesus, the risen Lord **who laid down His life** for us all, has the ability to be that **perfect friend.**

He's always "at your side...when you're down and out, when you're on the street...sailing right behind." He's that friend "when friends just can't be found." No earthly friend fills that bill. No one but Jesus is always at our side, caring, loving, and able to bring about all the song expresses. "Like a bridge over troubled water, I will lay me down." He laid Himself down on the wood of the cross to join earth again to heaven and you and me to God—and, with His arms outstretched, to join us to one another in and through Him. His self-giving love is alive and completely unchanging. Even in the best of friendships between us human beings, there can sometimes be a wavering, a growing hot or cold. Besides that, we're all going to die, but the friendship of Jesus is an adventure for a lifetime and for eternity.

I told that once to a tough teenager, after running out of other things to say. He was all broken up himself after having just broken up with his girlfriend. I thought it missed him by a mile. I found out that later he was talking to his buddies, telling them, "Hey man! There's only one friend you can always count on, and that's Jesus."

Once I was flat on my back in a hospital bed. I had difficulty getting my thoughts together enough to pray, but I had my Bible

Who Is Jesus Christ?

with me. I used to have a custom of asking God to guide me each day to something to read. I opened the Scriptures and read these words at the end of the second chapter of Paul to the Galatians. *"I still live my human life, but it's a life of faith in the Son of God who loved me and gave Himself for me"* (NAB unrevised edition). The words went right through my heart. I had probably read them many times, but that's one reason why we sometimes get knocked down. It's so that God can get our attention and we can find out that He's the one who lifts us up. That day, I heard those words in a way that I had never heard them before. What I heard was that He loved **me** and gave Himself **for me**. And I said, "Wow!"

Everything that Jesus did—when He was born, when He walked this earth, when He taught, when He gave us His body and blood, when they whipped Him and drove the spikes into His hands and feet, when He hung there in agony for three hours—He did for me. Yes, *He did it for everyone, but if I had been the only one in the whole world, His love is great enough that He would have gone through it just for me*. He loves me that much, not just two thousand years ago, but right now. At this moment, the love that brought Jesus to the cross burns in His heart for me.

At Mass, when I'm invited to come up to Holy Communion, Jesus is offering me His Body, His Blood, His Soul, His Divinity, and His Holy Spirit. He is saying, "I did it for you, and I love you that much—not just when you go to Communion—but in this sacrament, I'm giving you the sign, the embodiment of the love I have for you every day, every moment. That's how much I love you. Would you just open your heart, believe it, receive it, and love me and others in return? I'm your friend; would you be mine? Would you walk down the road of life with me? Would you share all your ups and downs with me? Would you bring me all your struggles, dreams, and plans? Would you let me lead and guide and use you all along the way, willing to '*do what I command you*'?" An anonymous author has captured the heart of this in an imaginative "Letter to a Friend."

> I just had to write to tell you how much I love you and care for you. Yesterday, I saw you walking and laugh-

ing with your friends. I hoped that, soon, you'd want me to walk along with you, too. So I painted you a sunset to close your day and whispered a cool breeze to refresh you. I waited; you never called. I just kept on loving you.

As I watched you fall asleep last night, I wanted so much to reach out to you. I spilled moonlight onto your face—trickling down your cheeks as so many tears have. You didn't think of me; I wanted so much to comfort you.

The next day, I exploded a brilliant sunrise into a glorious morning for you, but you woke up late and rushed off to work—you didn't even notice. My sky became cloudy, and my tears were the rain.

I love you. Oh, if you'd only listen. I **really** love you!!! I try to say it in the quiet of the green meadows and in the blue sky. The wind whispers my love throughout the treetops and spills it into the vibrant colors of all the flowers. I shout it to you in the thunder of the great waterfalls and compose love songs for birds to sing to you. I warm you with the clothing of sunshine and perfume the air with nature's sweet scent. My love for you is deeper than any ocean and greater than any need in your heart. If you'd only realize how I care!!

My Dad sends His love. I want you to meet Him—He cares so. Fathers are just that way. So, **please call on me** soon. No matter how long it takes, I'll wait, because I love you!!!

Your Friend, Jesus

MY SAVIOR

"Miserable one that I am! Who will deliver me…? Thanks be to God through Jesus Christ our Lord" (Rom 7:24-25).

Jesus Christ is our great brother and friend. He is also our Savior. Do you know you need a Savior? A lot of people think they don't. A survey of Christian churchgoers was made in a certain area of our country. Its results were amazing. It found that many, if not the majority, thought they didn't need a Savior. They thought other people needed Him, but not them! Now, I can identify with that, because there were years of my life when that's where I was. I thought other people needed a Savior. I thought the guy I was working with needed a Savior, but I didn't know how much **I** needed Him.

I was on a retreat once, and, though I can't remember exactly who the preacher was (I think it was a Catholic bishop from Kentucky), God used him to break through to me. Ever since then, I can say with the old spiritual, "It's not my brother or my sister, but it's **me**, O Lord, standing in the need of prayer." I don't know about the other guy, but I know, Lord, I need you, and I need you every day.

I know that there are things lurking inside of me, things that are the result of original sin and my own sins—like pride, self-centeredness, laziness, etc., and, if I didn't open my life day after day to Jesus Christ, they would ruin me. I know that there are temptations that come at me every day, and, without the grace of Jesus Christ, I would fall flat on my face over and over. I know I have a free will, but I also know the temptations of this world would do me in if it weren't for His grace.

I know too that I need Him every moment in my mission as a Christian and a priest. I want to touch people's lives and bring about true change, but I don't have that power. I could talk until I'm blue in the face. People might go away and—if they're polite—say, "That was nice," but it wouldn't make a bit of difference in their souls or their way of life. I can't make the difference. I can't get inside—but **He** can. As some of my black brothers and sisters put it, He's the "heart-fixer and the mind-regulator." He's *"the vine;"* we're *"the branches"* (Jn 15:1-10). He can use me, and He can use you, but it's only His saving grace and the response to it that will get the job done. *"I planted,"* Paul said. *"Apollos watered, but God caused the growth"* (1Cor 3:6). Jesus alone is the Savior. None of us are.

At the end of the 7th chapter of Paul's letter to the Romans, he says, *"I discover the principle that when I want to do right, evil is at hand. For I take delight in the law of God, in my inner self, but I see in my members another principle at war with the law of my mind, taking me captive to the law of sin that dwells in my mem-*

bers." Is it difficult to understand what Paul is saying? He says that there are things that I want to do with my mind; there are good resolutions that I make, but there is something else going on inside of me that interferes with carrying out all those good desires and resolutions. Is there anyone who can't identify with that?

Anne Frank, the Jewish teenager who died in a Nazi concentration camp, writes about that struggle in the last few pages of her diary.

> I'm split in two....My...superficial side will always steal a march on the deeper side and therefore always win....How often I've tried to push away this Anne, to...hide her. But it doesn't work....I'm afraid that people who know me...will discover I have...a better side. I'm afraid they'll mock me....So the nice Anne is never seen in company....because (I) don't listen to the advice of (my) own better half....I...end up turning my heart inside out, the bad part on the outside and the good part on the inside, and keep trying to find a way to become what I'd like to be and what I could be if...if only....

She echoes the cry of people around the world who have experienced that rebellion ever since the fall of Adam and Eve. It's the evidence that a monkey-wrench was thrown into the works at the very dawn of humanity. Sin entered the world, and we still bear the consequences of original sin. With St. Paul, we can all say, "*Miserable one that I am, who will deliver me...?*" Let the whole world listen to the answer: "*Thanks be to God through Jesus Christ Our Lord!*" (Rom 7:24-25).

Jesus alone has that saving power. He alone can win the victory—the ultimate victory over death and the day-by-day victory over sin. Without Jesus, we would be ruined. Without the grace of Jesus Christ, none of us would make it to the goal of eternal life. No matter how good we think we are, no matter what good acts we do, it is only through Jesus Christ that we're saved. Refusing to do good and avoid serious sin blocks out His saving grace, but ultimately salvation is His free gift.

Grace is to us what oxygen is to the astronauts. When they go into outer space, a completely different atmosphere awaits them. Astronauts can't live in that airless environment. They have to bring the oxygen with them to survive. If we somehow got into heaven without the sanctifying grace of Jesus Christ, we couldn't live the life of heaven. We wouldn't survive. It's a different life, a supernatural life, and we're not equipped for it unless we have that life in us before we leave this earth—and that's a free gift of God. Unlike oxygen, His grace inwardly transforms us *"So whoever is in Christ is a new creation…"* (2 Cor 5:17). It's also only through His on-going help that we can take the steps in this life that ultimately lead to life everlasting.

That Jesus is our Savior means He has the power not just to save us from sin in a narrow sense but also from the effects of sin. He can free us from fears and anxieties, from hang-ups and addictions, from hurtful memories and strained relationships, as well as from our physical illnesses. He demonstrated this many times when He walked among us.

God powerfully uses Sister Briege McKenna, O.S.C., in the healing ministry. Through the years, He has taught her what the great medieval theologian, St. Thomas Aquinas, maintained: **the Holy Eucharist is the greatest healing sacrament**. The first time I ever heard Sister Briege address a group of priests in New Orleans, she told a story that brought tears to my eyes. There was a young priest with throat cancer so advanced that they planned to perform a laryngectomy and take out his voice box, leaving only a little hole in his throat. Depressed at the prospect of the operation, he put in a long-distance call to Sister Briege and begged her to come, lay hands on him in the name of Jesus, and pray for a healing of his throat.

She said, "Father, I'm sorry, but I can't come; however, I'll tell you what you can do. Tomorrow morning when you stand at the altar and consecrate the bread that becomes the Body of Jesus and receive Holy Communion, ask Jesus, who healed the blind and the lame, to touch your throat. When you drink from the Cup of Salvation that becomes His Blood, ask Jesus, by the power of His Blood, to heal that cancer."

The next morning, he did that in simple faith. Sometime afterwards, he went back to the doctor, probably for the last examination before the surgery. The doctor examined him very carefully and said something like, "Father, I can't believe what I'm seeing. You won't need that operation. Your throat is healed!"

Certainly, physical healings like this are not the most important ones, and they don't always happen. Suffering in union with Christ has its own salvific value, and grace for this is itself a healing gift. Nevertheless, when we come to Jesus in prayer and especially in the sacraments He gave us, we're coming to Him who said, *"I am the resurrection and the life"* (Jn 11:25). He has the power to give new life in body, in mind, in heart, in memory, and above all, in our inner spirit. He has come to lift up a fallen world now and forever and to restore us to the dignity of God's sons and daughters. In every sense, He is truly our Savior.

JESUS CHRIST IS LORD
*"...every knee should bend...
and every tongue confess that Jesus Christ is Lord..."*
(Phil 2:11).

Jesus Christ is also Lord of our lives. On that first Pentecost Sunday when Peter stood up in the streets of Jerusalem and proclaimed the Good News publicly for the first time since the Ascension, he ended his sermon with the cry, *"Therefore let the whole house of Israel know for certain that God has made both Lord and Messiah this Jesus whom you crucified"* (Acts 2:36).

Is He the Lord of your life? That's the crucial question in our relationship with Jesus Christ. That's where "the rubber hits the road." It's easy enough to accept Jesus as a brother and a friend. It's nice to be able to turn to Him as Savior, especially in time of trouble, but **the key question remains—is He my Lord? Have I turned everything over to Him and surrendered my life to Him?**

In my radio ministry, I occasionally have interviews. One was with Danny Abramowitz, a former star of the New Orleans Saints football team. Danny told the story of how he won the NFL title of Number One pass-receiver one year. Then, when he left the Saints, he said to himself, "Well, I made it big with the Saints, so now I'm going to make it big in the business world as well." So he did, but, in his own personal life and in his marriage and family, things were all messed up because of an abuse of alcohol.

One morning, he woke up, looked at himself in the mirror, and was disgusted with what he saw. He talked to a priest and, subsequently, got into an AA program. Some time after that, he attended a "Life in the Spirit" seminar sponsored by the Catholic Charismatic Movement during which there was a talk about the Lordship of Jesus. The person giving the talk had drawn three circles on a chalkboard representing each of us and, next to or in the circles, crosses which represented Jesus.

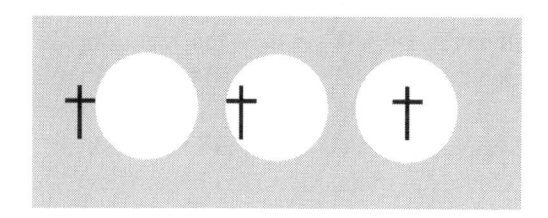

† ○ † ○ † ○

The speaker explained that the first circle (with the cross right on the outside) represented those who say they believe in Jesus, but He's not involved in their daily lives. He's out there somewhere, but, for them, His existence makes little or no difference. They live pretty much the same as if they didn't believe in Jesus. The second circle, with the cross right on the inside edge, represents those who believe in Jesus. He's involved in their lives, but only peripherally. He's not the center or Lord of their lives. The third circle, with the cross smack in the center, represents those who try to let Jesus be Lord and center of their existence.

In the interview, Danny said something like this: "That night, when I was looking at those three circles, I focused on the second one with the cross on the inside—but right on the edge. I said to myself, 'That's me; that's Danny.' I believe in Jesus. I'm Catholic. He's in my life. I go to church. I pray when I'm in trouble, but He's not the center of my life. Who is? It's me; it's Danny. I'm Number One. I do things to please myself, even in my marriage and family. My abuse of alcohol is for my kicks, even though it's ruining my life. My business—it's for me to get ahead. My time, my talents, my money—it's all for me. But, beginning right now, I want to change all that. I want to get out of the center and invite Jesus to take over. I want to ask Him to show me how to be a husband to my wife and a father to my children. I want to ask Him what He wants me to do with my business, my time, my talent, my money—with everything. It all comes from Him, and, in one moment, He could take it all away. I want to release it to Him and let Him be the Lord of it all."

Danny has a great sense of humor. He says, "You know, when you say that to the Lord, you don't know if you really mean it! That's why you have to keep saying it every day of your life, hoping that, as time goes on, you will mean it more and more."

I can still picture myself, sitting in that recording booth at WWL radio, listening to this guileless man tell his story. I remember how moved I was. His testimony triggered in me a memory of a retreat I had made years after I had gotten to know Jesus in a more personal way. On that particular retreat, I began to realize how much of my own life was centered around myself and my success. I wanted to be somebody, and I was (at least subconsciously) even using the priesthood to achieve it. I remembered going to Jesus and telling Him, "Forgive me, Lord, I've got it backwards. It's not my success, but your success, not my kingdom I want to build, but yours. From now on, I don't care anymore whether or not I succeed as long as you do. Even if I make a fool out of myself, Lord, it's all right. Just use me and let your Kingdom come."

I recall that when I said that, it was like a weight of years being lifted from my shoulders. I had been set free. **But**, as Danny says, you need to **keep** saying it, because the temptation is always there to take it back. Also, when you say something like, "I don't care even if I make a fool out of myself," you better mean it, because He might take you up on it! He has for me.

I don't think it was long after that retreat that I was invited to give a mission in a little town in southern Alabama. As I prepared for the opening night, I remember getting nervous and uptight, probably because I was again concerned about success, including how I would go over and the impression I would make. I mapped out

Who Is Jesus Christ?

the opening talk on a laminated sheet (something I hardly ever do) and also brought a chalkboard into the sanctuary. The first thing to go wrong that night was that the board was at one end of the sanctuary and the stationary mike was at the other. I had to keep running back and forth between the board and the mike, feeling and looking like a jack-in-the-box. Also, they had given me a little piece of chalk, and I scraped the board a number of times either with the chalk or my fingernail, sending chills down everybody's spine. At one point, I had to erase the board, but there was no eraser, so I ended up using my Mass vestments instead. To cap it all, I looked down and noticed that both of my shoes were untied, so, in full view of the congregation, I bent over and tied them.

Sitting towards the front of the church was a teenage girl who was watching me, wide-eyed. The next day, I happened to see her somewhere in town, and she came up to me excitedly and said, "Hey Father, I really enjoyed your talk last night—especially that part where you tied your shoes!" I guess she figured, "That guy's all right. He doesn't have it all together any more than the rest of us!"

God used my foolishness that night to get through to her. *"God chose the foolish of the world to shame the wise"* (1 Cor. 1:27). He wants to use each of us; we just need to let Him.

In the last parish where I served as pastor, I received a young doctor into the Catholic Church. He had been to churches of many different religious denominations, but he had never been baptized. The day he came to Mass for the first time in a Catholic church, he told me that he experienced the presence of Jesus Christ in a way he had never before known. It was Jesus in the Holy Eucharist who drew him into the Catholic faith. He received instructions, and I baptized him, but then he moved away. Years later, I met him again; I think it was in South Dakota. He told me, "Father, you know that business of letting Jesus be the Lord of your life? That's really something!" He described for me just one day in his life as a doctor, when he woke up in the morning and said, "Jesus, this is your day. Just use me." He told me how, on that one day, God used him, including ways that were very simple and undramatic. That young doctor taught me something. In my prayers every morning now, I add that petition: "Jesus, this is your day. Just use me."

Let me ask you this, but take your time in answering. Are you afraid to let Jesus be the Lord of your life? Are you afraid to say, "Jesus, here is my time, my talents, my money, and my relationships. Here's everything. Just show me what you want me to do with it all, and give me the grace to do it."

Are you afraid to say that? Do you ever get afraid? Do you ever hesitate, even for a moment? Who doesn't! Of course we get afraid and sometimes hesitate, but why? We're afraid of what He might ask of us—of what He might want us to do. Let me ask you this: would He ever ask anything wrong of you? Is there anyone who truly loves you more than He and has at heart all that is best for you? Is there anyone who knows better than He what will truly bring you the deepest peace and joy? Is there anyone who can bring it about more than He?

Then, why should any of us let fear keep us from saying to Him, *"Lord, here I am. Take my time, my talents, my family, my work, my everything. You have given it all to me. In one moment, you could take it all away. I entrust it all to you. Just show me what you want me to do with it and use me in the short time of my life that I have left to reach out to others in your name. From this day forward, I'm yours. Just lead me, Lord, guide me, and use me. All you holy ones who have gone before me following Him, Mary and the saints—and all you angels—pray for me all along the way."*

Around the world, the Catholic Church proclaimed a theme for the Jubilee year 2000, the beginning of this new millennium: "Open Wide the Doors to Christ." What a different world it would be if all nations, institutions, and peoples would heed that cry. What a different life if you and I lived it. At the end of the 3rd chapter of the Book of Revelation, there is the image of Jesus knocking at a door saying, *"Behold, I stand at the door and knock. If anyone hears my voice and opens the door,* (then) *I will enter his home and dine with him, and he, with me"* (v 20). That door is your heart, your life, and mine. He's always knocking; He doesn't force His way in. He waits for us to keep opening the door wider and wider.

Something you can do often, especially after Holy Communion but at other times as well, is close your eyes and picture your

Who Is Jesus Christ?

heart as that door, with Jesus knocking. In your imagination, if you so choose, open the door and invite Him in. You could pray this prayer:

> Lord, all the love in the world is just a sample of your love for me. I welcome you as **brother, friend**, and **bridegroom**. I never need to walk alone. I can share all my ups and downs with you and let every day be "a closer walk" with you. I open the door to you also as **Savior**. You died for me as if I were the only one. Forgive me, Lord, all my sins. I'm sorry for offending you, who are so good and deserving of all my love. Deliver me from evil. Break the chains of addictions, compulsions, and destructive habits of thought or action. Unbind me and let me go free. Give me that particular grace that I need. Fill me with your Holy Spirit. Deepen my faith, my hope, my surrender, my love. Finally, Jesus, I open the door to you as my **Lord and God**. All that I am and have comes from you. I lay it down at your feet and want to use it only the way you want me to use it. Use me, Lord, to reach out to others in your name.
> AMEN

Love's the Message that I Heard

CHAPTER 3

The Prayer That Pierces The Clouds And Hearts
*How's and Why's of
Personal and Communal Prayer*

Part I
Personal Prayer
"He was praying in a certain place, and when he had finished, one of his disciples said to him, 'Lord, teach us to pray'" (Lk 11:1).

To be effective in our lives as Christians, we need to be people of prayer. But even for this, we depend on God's grace, so let's ask Him right now: *"**Lord, teach us to pray.**"*

In my first pastorate, one of the most active parishioners had a keen interest in the whole field of solar energy—the science of how to capture the power of the sun to warm buildings, run generators, operate furnaces, etc. I think of prayer as something like that. Prayer is the way that you and I capture the power of God to energize and transform our lives and, in turn, to become transformers in this world of ours.

When we read the lives of the saints, we meet people who were fragile human beings, just like the rest of us. What made them different was that they learned the secret of how to open themselves, day by day, to the transforming power of God, especially in prayer. Pope John Paul II puts it this way: "Christians are worth as much as they pray."

Some people say, "**You** do the praying; **I'll** do the working. I'm a person of action; you can be the pray-er." Well, unless you have a special vocation to a life of contemplation, it's not either/or; it's both/and. For your work to be effective for God's kingdom, it needs to be backed up by prayer. On the other hand, if your

55

prayer is honest and wholehearted, it will inevitably have an effect on your life and work. Looking at Jesus, we see a life that was both contemplative and active. As we open ourselves to Him more and more in daily life, and especially in prayer, we become ever more the instruments of His mission. *"I am the vine, you are the branches. Whoever remains in me and I in him will **bear much fruit**, because without me you can do nothing"* (Jn 15:5).

SO WHY PRAY?

Others say, "My prayers aren't answered. I prayed for this or that, but I never got it." Every good prayer has an effect. The first effect is in our own lives and in our own hearts. Prayer is an opening of our hearts to God, and, when we sincerely do that, something happens.

Why do we pray? It's not primarily to get this or that. We pray, first of all, to get God. We pray for the same reason we talk to those we love. What we say isn't as important as the fact that we are talking to each other. We're communicating, and that communication brings us together. Of course, the more open, honest, and heartfelt the communication is, the closer we become. When we pray, **it's so that we can be brought into a closer union with God.** Union with Him is joy now and will be our joy for all eternity. *"Remain in my love…that my joy may be in you and your joy be complete"* (Jn 15:9 & 11). That union is the goal of our existence, and the degree of joy—even in heaven—will be in proportion to how much we have grown in loving union with Him in this life. That's the first purpose—and the main purpose—of prayer.

FROM THE HEART

The most important thing to emphasize about prayer is that it be from our hearts and not just our lips. *"Don't babble like the pagans,"* Jesus says (Mt 6:7).

There's a joke about the guy who went to confession and, for his penance, was asked to pray the Acts of Faith, Hope, and Charity. (Don't worry. Priests don't usually suggest that.)

The Prayer That Pierces The Clouds And Hearts

After a pause and a few coughs, the poor fellow said, "Father, I used to know those prayers, but I forgot them. Could you give me something else?"

"Okay," said the priest, "pray the Apostles' Creed." (This is also not a usual penance.)

There was another pause, a few more coughs, and then, "Father, I used to know that prayer, but I forgot it. Would you give me something else?"

"Well then," said the priest, "pray the Our Father three times."

This time, there was a long pause and the poor guy said, "Father, I'm really embarrassed to tell you this. I know the first part of the Our Father, but I get mixed up on the second. Could you give me something else?"

The priest scratched his head and asked, "Hey, do you know any prayers at all?"

"Yeah," the man said, "I know the Angelus."

(In case you're not familiar with it, the Angelus is the prayer commemorating the great moment of the Incarnation, when the angel appeared to Mary and announced that God's time had come and that she was to be the Mother of the Lord (Lk 26-38). It is prayed in many places around the world with the ringing of the church bells at 6:00 in the morning, 12:00 noon, and 6:00 in the evening.)

Anyway, the priest was amazed that, of all prayers, this fellow knew the Angelus—a comparatively long and complicated prayer with three verses and responses. The priest exclaimed, "You know the Angelus?"

"Yeah," the man answered.

"Well, pray the Angelus," the priest said.

So the man went out and started fulfilling his penance.

Before the priest left to go back to the rectory, he happened to kneel down a few pews behind the man, close enough to hear him. What he was praying as he rhythmically struck his chest was, "Bong...bong...bong...!" The point is that sometimes our prayer can be just going through the motions.

Of course, we're all distracted at times in prayer; that's human. As long as you want to pray and you keep trying to pray from your heart, God honors that.

Some years ago, I saw a movie called *Without a Trace*. It's based on a true story about a child who gets kidnapped in a large city like New York. In the opening scene, the little boy is getting ready for school as his mother (separated at the time from her husband) fixes his breakfast and has a typical morning conversation with him. They leave the house together, and she leads him down the street. The little boy turns the corner to his school, and his mother waves good-bye and goes off to work.

That evening when she comes home, the little boy is not there. She figures, "Well, he must have stopped at the house of a little friend." She calls, but he's not there. It gets dark, and the child still has not come home. She realizes that her son is lost in this large city. She calls the police, and the search begins. The drama of the movie is around this search for a lost child.

There is a scene in the movie where the mother is preparing to go to sleep and turns out the light beside her bed. For a few moments on the screen there is total darkness and absolutely no sound. As I sat in the theater, I thought that something had gone wrong with the projection camera. Then, out of the darkness, come the words, *"I believe in God, the Father Almighty, Creator of heaven and earth..."* Just those few words, possibly the beginning of a mother's rosary, are heard. Then the scene changes, and it's the next day, but those brief words of prayer in that setting have such an intense effect. They help to remind us of the power and beauty of even a few words of prayer, if they really come from the heart. That's the kind of prayer that changes our hearts and that God accepts to change the world around us.

FIVE ASPECTS OF PRAYER

Prayer is more than intercession. Actually, there are five major aspects to prayer. Somewhere along the line, I picked up a little memory aid to help recall them (and when you get older, that helps!) Take the word "**ALTAR**." Each letter of the word represents one of the aspects of prayer.

"**A**" **is for Adoration.** God is the only one whom I adore.

The Prayer That Pierces The Clouds And Hearts

Some people say, "I adore this hat," or "I adore that child," but that's just an expression. God is the only one who deserves true adoration. Before God, I fall down and acknowledge, "Everything I am and everything I have comes from You. I want to use it all according to the way you want. You are the Lord. You are my God." The greatest act of public adoration is in the Mass itself, because it is the complete surrender of Jesus to the Father and our surrender along with Him; however, we can also express adoration privately in our personal prayer. Even to genuflect or kneel in prayer is an act of adoration.

"**L**" **is for Love.** Prayer is an act of love. In prayer, I'm getting in touch with the love that is at the center of the universe. It is God's love that created and sustains everything and which redeems and saves us. I'm opening myself to that love, exercising an act of love for Him, and hopefully growing in my capacity to love God and neighbor. When I pray for others, it's an act of love as well.

"**T**" **is for Thanksgiving and Praise.** Through so much of my life, I've asked God for things. Before I die, I hope that I will have caught up and thanked Him as much as I've asked Him. Ideally, I'll go beyond that. As the beautiful old song, "Blessed Assurance" expresses it: "This is my story; this is my song, praising the Savior, all the day long." I hope thanksgiving will continue to grow in my life, and that, one day in my heart, I will be "praising the Savior all the day long" for everything—even for difficulties and troubles, trusting that He's at work in them as well.

"**A**" **is for Asking.** I have a friend—a good man—who used to say, "I don't know why I should ask God for anything. He already knows. I can thank Him, but why should I ask?" I don't know the complete answer to that, but I do know that Jesus said, *"Ask, and you shall receive. Seek, and you shall find. Knock, and the door will be opened to you"* (Lk. 11:9). I also know from experience—mine and others—that when we ask, things begin to happen. People down through the ages have testified to that. God honors prayers of petition. I think it's because such prayers acknowledge that we depend upon Him, and we dispose ourselves to receive what He wants to give.

I pray for big things: peace in the world, respect for all human

59

life, reconciliation between enemies, the unity of all Christians, the return of those who have drifted from His Church, my on-going conversion, and the conversion of the world. I also pray for little things, as when I lose stuff (which I'm often doing). People laugh at me, but I'm regularly asking St. Anthony to pray for me to find them. (That's his specialty, you know.) It's amazing. I'll look somewhere, and it's not there. Then, I'll pray and look again in the same place, and there it is! It's as if God puts it there or at least opens my eyes to see what I didn't see before. In any case, He keeps me humbly dependent on Him and (figuratively) on my knees. I think that's one reason He lets me lose all those things!

Then finally, "R" is for Reparation. A popular romantic movie had a famous line: "Love means never having to say you're sorry"—famous but stupid. Among us sinful, fragile, human beings, love better learn how to say, "I'm sorry." We need to acknowledge our failings and ask forgiveness in our relationships with God and with one another. By prayer too, we can take steps to make up for the times we have offended and neglected Him and others, making amends for our own failures in love and that of our brothers and sisters.

So, if you're ever at prayer and at a loss for something to say, just recall the word "**ALTAR**." Make acts of adoration, love, thanksgiving, asking, or reparation. The various aspects of prayer are more adequately treated in the official 1993 Catechism of the Catholic Church. In fact, the fourth and final section of the Catechism is entirely devoted to the subject of prayer. It is probably the finest compilation of wisdom and helpful insights on the subject from the Scriptures, the writings of the early Church Fathers, and the Saints.

PRACTICES OF PRAYER

In the modern Church, many people neglect the practice of set times for prayer in their daily lives. Some of us, however, grew up with a regular routine of prayer. We said morning prayers, night prayers, meal prayers, the rosary, and maybe even the Angelus! "But I don't want to be tied down to all that routine," some say.

The Prayer That Pierces The Clouds And Hearts

"That's too mechanical. I'll pray when I feel moved to or when the Spirit hits me." In his little book on prayer, Karl Rahner—whose theological tracts are often pretty heavy and dense but whose spiritual writings are different—deals with this modern attitude in surprisingly simple and forthright terms. His response can be boiled down to one word: "Baloney!" We humans, he reminds us, need certain routines, regular practices, and habits of life.

Most of us eat three meals a day, don't we? That's a routine! We usually enjoy it, and we know we need it. Well, **whether we feel like it or not, we need to pray.** God always deserves our worship, and we require it for our own spiritual survival and growth. In fact, when we think we're on top of everything and don't need God, that's when we're in the greatest danger! *"Therefore, whoever thinks he is standing secure should take care not to fall"* (1 Cor 10:12).

On the other hand, when the feelings have gone and prayer is as dry as dust, don't ever give it up! Unless you're putting some block to God in your life, the dryness could be a time of true progress in prayer and an occasion of deep purification. The saints experienced it—often for long periods of time. In the words of the old spiritual masters, it's a call to *"seek not so much the consolations of God as to seek the God of consolations."*

Begin each day with the sign of the cross and prayer. I still go down on my knees when I get out of bed. That's an act of prayer in itself. I don't usually get on my knees for anybody else. It expresses the offering of myself, my whole body and soul, to God. If your knees don't permit it, He accepts you just as you are. A doctor friend told me that, for people over forty, it would be less strain on the heart to begin prayer (and some simple exercise) in bed for a short while before attempting to get up. End the day with prayer— at least a brief review of the daily events with gratitude to God and repentance for sins. (It's also a good way to exercise the memory.) You might specifically thank God for three blessings of that day and possibly write them down in your own "book of blessings." This could be followed by an act of contrition out of love for Him as we look at a crucifix—the great image of His love and sacrifice.

Meals are a special occasion for families to pray and give thanks together. To do it individually is also good. It doesn't always have to be a set prayer; it can be spontaneous. I remember a time I was invited to someone's home for dinner and was asked to offer the "Grace Before Meals." I just prayed a spontaneous prayer from my heart, and a little boy in the family piped up with, "Hey Mom, is that the new Catholic Grace?"

The rosary is a beautiful prayer for every day. If you're not accustomed to praying it, you might start with only one decade. Carry it in your pocket or purse and take it to bed with you at night. Just to have it with you is a great reminder of Jesus, Mary, and the cross of our salvation. There are so many miracles of grace and conversions that have come from praying the rosary. God has also confirmed its value with healings and with apparitions of Our Lady.

When the church bells ring at 6:00 AM, noon, or 6:00 PM, we're invited to pray the Angelus or at least a Hail Mary or just to thank God for the great mystery of the Word made Flesh. I've rediscovered the Angelus as a most appropriate prayer to intercede for the life of the unborn and a return to respect for every human life.

The three o'clock hour, the hour of His crucifixion and our redemption, is also a fitting time to plead for our conversion and that of the whole world. Many people are now praying "the Divine Mercy Chaplet," which mainly consists of repeating "*For the sake of His sorrowful passion, have mercy on us and on the whole world*" on the rosary beads.

MEDITATIVE PRAYER

There is a book by a Catholic psychologist, Dr. DeBlassie, called *Inner Calm,* which is now, unfortunately, out of print. One of the ways to this inner calm that the doctor recommends is to take at least twenty minutes in the morning and another twenty minutes in a latter part of the day as a quiet time of prayer. Specifically, he suggests that the time be used to relax completely, to focus your attention on Our Lord, and, as you breathe deeply and rhythmically, to say over and over "***Lord***" (breathing in), "***Jesus***" (breathing out). He cites actual cases of the tranquilizing influence of this type of prayer in the lives of formerly very anxious people.

Anxious or not, we all need a quiet time of prayer in our daily lives if we want to make progress in our relationship with God. This is especially true for those of us who are daily assaulted by noise, rush, and busyness. My own experience has been that such time is invaluable and results in a better, more efficient use of the rest of the hours of the day and more effective action for the Lord.

I think of the testimony I heard years ago from Father Michael Scanlan, the Chancellor of Franciscan University of Steubenville, Ohio. God used him to turn that university into one of the best Catholic universities in our country. The secret behind it was a decision about prayer.

Besides his many other activities, Father Scanlan regularly spent from 8:00 AM until noon taking care of the school's business. Somewhere along the line, he began to realize that he needed to take more time for prayer. So, he started setting aside two hours each day, from 8:00 AM to 10:00 AM, for reading Scripture and for prayer. What he noticed as he began to do this was that he was able to accomplish between 10:00 AM and noon all that he had previously done between 8:00 AM and noon! Giving those two hours to prayer not only didn't cause him to get behind in his work, it actually allowed him to do it better, faster, and more effectively. Time used in genuine prayer is not wasted. Without shirking our responsibilities, we end up doing what we're called to do all the better.

Some say, "I pray always" or "My work is my prayer," so why do we need a special time or place? Paul urges us: *"Rejoice always. Pray without ceasing. In all circumstances give thanks, for this is the will of God for you in Christ Jesus"* (1 Thes 5:16-18). To pray always is the goal to strive for. A help to this is to cultivate living in the presence of God and in the present moment, doing everything *"...from the heart as for the Lord"* (Col 3:23). "He who performs the duties of his calling," says St. Francis de Sales, "with diligent care for the love of God, is truly pious and a man after God's heart."

It helps, too, to have a prayer, a song, or just the name of Jesus in our minds and hearts throughout the day. We're usually kidding ourselves when we think we can sustain this kind of prayer without the discipline of a daily, special, quiet time with Him. Even if we have arrived at praying always, there is still a difference between giving Him our full attention, which He deserves, and communicating with Him (or anyone) while we're engaged in some other distracting activity.

Take that quiet time with Him every day. An hour would not be too much. The night before He died, Jesus asked, *"Could you not keep watch for one hour?"* (Mk 14:37). We find in the Gospels that *"He went, as was his custom..."* to pray in the Garden of Gethsemane (Lk. 22:39). That's how Judas knew where to find Him; it was the tip-off. "It's like clockwork; you can count on it. You'll find Him praying alone at night in the Garden of Gethsemane." Jesus gives us an example of the regular use of a quiet time and place. It's important that you find that daily quiet place in your own heart, even if there's noise around you. If an hour scares you, start with a half hour. If a half hour scares you, start with ten minutes.

I mentioned that idea once at a parish mission long ago in Chauvin, a little town along Bayou Lafourche in South Louisiana. I went back to St. Joseph church years later, and a woman was giving a public testimony. I don't think she even knew I was there.

"Years ago, I made a mission," she said, "and I don't remember anything the missionary said—except for one thing. He said, 'Even if it's only ten minutes a day, take some quiet time with God.' I said to myself, 'I can do that,' and I went home and started to take ten minutes every day." She would set her kitchen timer.

That woman had all kinds of problems in her life and no personal relationship with the Lord at the time, but those ten minutes began to transform her. Now, she takes a lot more time than that, and God uses her in a most effective way in her community. It started with the simple decision to take ten minutes of prayer with the Lord each day.

Be faithful to that daily quiet time with Him, and, if brief, then build on it and increase it. If you can go before Our Lord in the Blessed Sacrament, that would be the best place of prayer. The

The Prayer That Pierces The Clouds And Hearts

Pope has expressed the hope for "the establishment of perpetual Eucharistic adoration in all parishes and Christian communities throughout the world" (Eucharistic Congress, June 1993, Seville, Spain). If you can't go to a church or chapel, then just pray anywhere. If the bathroom is the only quiet place in the house, use it! If driving to work, nursing or rocking the baby, washing dishes, or working on the assembly line is the only time you can find—do what you can.

USING QUIET TIME

For those who wonder, "What would I do with that time?" there are books of meditations that could help. One such book is called *My Daily Bread* (Confraternity of the Precious Blood, Brooklyn, N.Y.). I gave it to a teenager, a football player who lived in the inner-city, African-American parish in New Orleans where I was pastor. He told me later that that little book changed his life. Although not particularly geared to teenagers, the book has a wide appeal. It's modeled on brief conversations between you and the Lord for every day. You read it, reflect on it, and then continue the conversation on your own. Other such books are *My Daily Meditation on the Gospels* from the same publisher and several small volumes from Scepter Press called *In Conversation with God*, which are based on the Scripture readings from each day's Mass.

Of course, the best book is the Bible itself. Read it slowly, especially the Gospels. When something strikes you, close the book and let that sink in like a seed falling on the soil of your heart and taking root. Think about it. Talk to God about it. When that stops, read a little more, and then repeat the process. This meditative, prayerful reading of the Scriptures or other solid spiritual literature has a long tradition in the Church. It's called *"Lectio Divina"* or sacred reading.

Basically, when you pray, you're just opening your heart to God. We all know how to talk. Why can't we just talk to God? I once heard a Trappist monk say, *"Prayer is just honesty before God."* That's pretty simple, isn't it?

Years ago, I was invited to give a retreat for nuns. I had never done that before, and I wondered what to say. They were teaching nuns, and, when I talked to them about prayer, I said, "Sisters, when you pray, just tell it like it is. If you had a hard day in school with the kids, you can say, `Lord, I had a hard day in school. I feel like I could strangle somebody.' Or, you could say, 'I'm tired. I'm fed up.' Whatever it is, just tell Him, even if it's, 'Lord, I think I'm falling in love with the milkman.'" When I said that, they roared with laughter. I thought it was funny, but I didn't think it was *that* funny. They told me afterwards that there was a really cute milkman that delivered milk to that convent! I was just trying to say that, when you pray, you don't have to use fancy words or pious phrases. Just be yourself and open your heart to Him.

The problem with prayer for many of us is not prayer but life. We don't connect the two. We're not being real with God. We hide from Him, like Adam and Eve in the garden after sin (Gen. 3: 8-10). There are embarrassing moments in our conversation with God. There are certain things we don't want to talk about—and those are probably the special things we need to talk about. He understands better than anyone else our sinfulness, our weakness, our coldness, our indifference, our doubts, our fears, and our resentments. The song "Just As I Am" expresses it: "*Just as I am, though tossed about, with many a conflict, many a doubt, fightings and fears within, without, O Lamb of God, I come*." Whatever's going on in your life, talk to Him about it. Then, be quiet and listen to what He wants to say to you.

LISTENING IN PRAYER

Many of us never listen in prayer. (Some of us never listen in other conversations either; we do all the talking!) That God wants to communicate with us in prayer is something many of us don't really believe. Actually, *He wants to communicate with us* more than we want to communicate with Him—normally just in the quiet of mind and heart.

I'm well aware that this is an area where we can be deceived. We might hear in prayer what **we** want to hear rather than what **He** wants to speak. Our own false images of God could also influence

The Prayer That Pierces The Clouds And Hearts

us. At times, we could even be hearing the promptings of Satan more than the Holy Spirit. Wise discernment is needed (1 Thes 5:19-21). St. Ignatius deals with this in his *Spiritual Exercises*. In serious matters, consultation with a good spiritual director who, as Ignatius would say, "thinks with the Church" could be called for. All these cautions, however, should not stop us from *listening to God in prayer.*

A number of years ago, I conducted a mission at St. Clare's Parish in Waveland, Mississippi, and the pastor asked me to have a session in church for the school children. Since it had been a good while since I had a congregation like that, I searched my mind for something to say to them. Deciding to talk about prayer, I asked those little children to close their eyes for just a moment, to picture Jesus standing there right in front of them, and to tell Him the deepest thing in their hearts. It was a large church, filled with children, but they got very quiet as they did this. After that, I told them to take one more minute and listen to what He wanted to say to them. Then I said, "Now, open your eyes and tell me how many of you heard Jesus say something?"

Thirty hands went up in the front pews where the first, second, and third graders were sitting. (Big kids don't hear anything!) I walked down the aisle and began to ask them, "What did Jesus say to you?" As they told me, I was so touched that I stopped and said, "Hey, I want the whole school to hear this!" There were about fifteen of them left. I brought them up to the microphone and let them tell everyone what Jesus had said to them.

Half of them said, "God said, 'I love you.'" Do you know how wonderful that is? I can tell you God loves you, and others can keep telling you God loves you, but when God says that to you personally, in the quiet of your own heart, that's worth more than a thousand people telling it to you! In one minute, those little children heard Jesus say that to them. One child said, "God said to forgive." Another said, "God said, 'I forgive you.'" One said, "God said, 'Go to church,'" and another, "Go to church every day," and still another, "Bring other people to church."

One little girl whose name was Samantha had no arms or legs; she came up to the mike on the stumps of her legs. I had to lift her

67

up to speak and was too distracted to hear what she had to say. I found out afterwards that Samantha said that God told her, "Pray for everybody in the whole wide world." What a wonder—a child without arms and legs being taught to forget herself and to think of others!

There was one black child in what otherwise looked like a totally white school. What that little boy said was so deep that it took me a couple of days to get its full impact. He said that God told him, "I give you my heart; be nice." In the Old Testament, God says through the prophet Ezekiel that the day will come when "*I will give you a new heart and place a new spirit within you, taking from your bodies your stony hearts and giving you natural hearts...you will be my people, and I will be your God*" (Ez 36:26-28). In the New Testament, Jesus says, "*Love one another as I have loved you*" (Jn 14:34). That little boy heard this message in a way he could understand.

I share this because, if God could communicate with those little children in just one minute, why can't He communicate with all of us even though He wants to? I believe that's part of what Jesus meant when He said, "*Unless you...become like children, you will not enter the kingdom of heaven*" (Mt 18:3). I told them, "God wants to speak to you." They believed me, and God did speak. They weren't faking it. In the quiet of their hearts, those children heard God—and so can each of us if we persevere and listen in humble, expectant faith.

It might not happen as quickly or in exactly the same way as it did for the children. St. Therese, the "Little Flower," said that, more often than during the times of prayer, new understandings and insights about what to do and say would come to her in the course of the day as she needed them. She had disposed her heart for them in prayer.

God speaks in many ways: through the events of life, through other people, and, uniquely, through His inspired word in Sacred Scripture, particularly when proclaimed in the assembly of His Church. He also speaks clearly and unmistakably in the solemn, official teachings of His Church. "*Whoever listens to you listens to me*" (Lk 10:16; see also Gal 1:18 & 2:2). **When what we think** we have heard in prayer is contrary to right reason or the guidance of His Church, we can rest assured it is not from Him.

FIVE ANTENNAE FOR PRAYER

There's a little book by Father John Powell, S.J., called *He Touched Me*. It's a gem but out of print. It's his own testimony of finding and developing a personal relationship with Jesus. Toward the end of the book, he gives some valuable suggestions about prayer. He describes what he calls five antennae, similar to an antenna on a television set, through which God communicates with us, and we, with Him.

The first antenna is our mind, which was the way those young children heard God. Over and over again as I go to pray, I have many things on my mind. How should I handle this situation or that? What should I say to this person? What should be my response to this problem? In prayer, I just try to give it to God—not figure it out all by myself. I try to release it to Him and be open to what He wants. At the end of that prayer time, some light and direction usually come. It might not be the whole answer but just the beginning of an answer—maybe the first small step. Sometimes, He seems to say, "*Wait.*" Regularly, He uses inaudible words in the quiet of my heart like He did with the little children, calling me to rejoice and assuring me of His love, His delight, and that He will be there every step of the way.

The second antenna is our will. Often we have a pretty good idea of what we need to do, but we don't have the strength to do it. We don't have the will, the courage, or the love that the task requires. We can go to God with our weakness and our emptiness. We bring that to Him and let Him fill us and strengthen us. We cry out to Him over and over from the depths of our hearts and admit our need, and He communicates with us through our will. It's like the prayer of Jesus in that fearful agony in the Garden where He prayed, "*Father...not my will but yours be done*" and an angel came "*to strengthen him*" (Lk 22:43).

Our imagination is the third antenna. When you pray, you can use your imagination. You can picture Jesus right there with you. For example, when you pray the rosary, you could imagine yourself with Him in each of the mysteries (e.g., as one of the shepherds kneeling at the manger). You could take various incidents from the Bible and place yourself in a scene with Jesus. Imagine you're the blind man at the side of the road as Jesus passes by, and you keep crying out, *"Jesus, Son of David, have mercy on me...I want to see"* (Mk 10:46-52). "I want to see life, myself, and You as You are."

I'm often on the road with the evangelization work that I do. Sometimes when I'm driving, I'll picture Jesus sitting in the passenger seat next to me. Whatever's on my mind, whatever's in my heart, I'll talk over with Him and then ask, "Jesus, what do you want to say about that?" A man who heard me relate that in one of my mission sermons met me months later and said, "You know, I'm a traveling salesman, and I used to be so lonely on the road all by myself. Now, I'm never alone. Jesus rides with me." That's using your imagination to build a relationship with Him.

Imagination can also be helpful in *"the healing of memories."* Many of us are troubled by sad or fearful recurring memories. In our imaginations, we can invite Jesus into those memories, one at a time. We can picture Him there with us when the incident occurred and let Him bring His peace, His love, and His forgiveness, while we listen to what He says and experience what He does in the situation.

The fourth antenna is memory. One way that God communicates in prayer is simply by reminding us of something in the past that He's already said or done. It could be the memory of a way He intervened in our lives a long time ago. It was wonderful at the time, and we were deeply grateful, but then we forgot all about it. During prayer, God might bring it back to mind when we're facing a similar situation in order to reassure us. He might also remind us of something we read, experienced, or heard in a sermon. When God helps us remember something like that, He's communicating through memory.

The last antenna is our emotions. When we're way up, or way down, or all tied up and not sure what's going on, we can go to God and unwind in His presence. He knows. We can say, "Lord, I

The Prayer That Pierces The Clouds And Hearts

don't know exactly why I'm feeling this way, but You do. Maybe You're trying to tell me something through the emotions I'm experiencing right now." There's that good old spiritual that says,

> Nobody knows the trouble I've seen.
> Nobody knows but Jesus.
> Nobody knows the trouble I've seen.
> Glory! Hallelujah!
> Sometimes, I'm up. Sometimes, I'm down.
> Sometimes, I'm almost to the ground.
> O yes, Lord. O yes, Lord.
> But, nobody knows the trouble I've seen.
> Nobody knows but Jesus.
> Nobody knows the trouble I've seen.
> Glory! Hallelujah!

Yes, Glory! Hallelujah! Somebody does know. Somebody does understand. A psychologist would say that to be truly heard and understood by another is one of the most liberating experiences there is. Jesus understands completely and can do something about it. We can go to Him any day, any time in prayer.

A QUIETING TECHNIQUE

Many years ago, Father Ed Farrell taught a group of us a technique for getting into that special quiet time with God. Through the years, I've found it invaluable, use it (at least in part) every day, and want to share it with you. It can be done in a matter of minutes, sitting erect in a chair or pew, or lying flat on your back on the floor. Your back should be almost flush against the chair or floor, your feet lined up together, and your hands, palms open, on your knees or by your side.

(1) Beginning with your feet, relax your body, slowly picturing and sensing all the tension draining out of your feet, then your legs, and then your back. To release the tension in your neck, turn your head around a few times in a circular motion and then up and down to "crack your neck." Using the tips of your fingers, momentarily press your eyelids to let the tension out of your eyes.

(2) With your eyes closed, sense the air touching the tips of your fingers and strain your ears to hear a distant sound—a bird singing, crickets calling, an auto horn blowing.

(3) Begin to breathe deeply, slowly, and rhythmically.

(4) Using your imagination, picture yourself collecting all your inner baggage, thoughts, plans, concerns, and emotions, like a bundle of clothes to be dropped into the wash. Gather up the bundle, carry it, and lay it down at the feet of Jesus, however you picture Him (on the cross, or standing there with His arms outstretched to you, as He is depicted in some images of the Sacred Heart). Lay that burden down at His feet. Let it go. Release it to Him, and then back away a bit, getting some distance from it. As you look into Jesus' eyes, let Him look into yours. Quietly, or silently in your heart, begin to call His name, "**Jesus...**" as you slowly breathe in and out.

(5) This could be continued or another similar short prayer could be repeated, such as the so-called Jesus Prayer: "*Lord Jesus Chist, Son of God, have mercy on me, a sinner,*" or the prayer of St. Alphonsus: "*I love you Jesus, my love. I love you more than myself. I repent with my whole heart for having offended you. Never permit me to separate myself from you again. Grant that I may love you always, and then do with me what is your will.*" Such repetitious prayer is not condemned by Our Lord but only vain or meaningless repetition (Mt 6:7). Jesus in Gethsemane "*prayed a third time, saying the same thing*" (Mt 26:44), and the blind beggar was heard as "*he kept calling out...Son of David, have pity on me!*" (Lk 18:39).

Note that steps 1 to 4 are simply an introduction to becoming quiet, but step 5 could end up consuming almost all of the time if you find it helpful for prayerful union with Our Lord. Don't fail to leave at least a little time towards the end specifically for listening to what He wants to say to you. Note also that all of the above and other suggestions in this chapter are only meant to be a help to prayer. Use what works for you. My old monk spiritual director used to say in his typical laconic style, "*Pray as you can, not as you can't.*" One way or the other, don't neglect to pray—and never give up the practice no matter what. (Lk 18:1-8; 21:36)

Remember, too, that people who have persevered in communication with God for many years will often be given the gift of greater and greater simplicity. The famous illustration of this is the story told by St. John Vianney, the pastor of Ars, about the old peasant who came to church every day and remained in prayer for a long period before Our Lord in the Blessed Sacrament. One day the priest said, "I regularly see you here at prayer but you use no book or rosary and your lips don't move. What do you say?" "I just look at Him," the old man answered, "and He looks at me!"

When I hear that, I think of an elderly husband and wife who might just sit on the porch together in the evening, holding hands as they watch the sun go down. Words are not necessary; everything is understood.

PART II
COMMUNITY AND SHARED PRAYER

Our Lord wants us to pray personally and privately. He said, *"When you pray, go to your room. Pray to your Father in secret, and your Father, who sees what no one sees, will answer you"* (Mt 6:6). Up to now, we've been talking mostly about this kind of prayer. On the other hand, He also taught us, by word and example, to pray with one another. *"For where two or three are gathered together in my name, there am I in the midst of them"* (Mt 18:20). Again, it's not either/or, but both/and. Christian prayer is both personal and communal.

A woman on a retreat I was conducting shared this experience. Her son had a chronic, aggravating, and debilitating foot rash. She took him to one doctor after the other. The foot problem would go away for a while, but it would come right back again. He was on his high school's baseball team at the time and was actually the best player. One day at practice, the coach said something like, "Fellows, we've got this special game tonight, but you know Johnny won't be playing just because of a foot rash!" The implication was that the rash was nothing and that Johnny was a sissy. When Johnny came home that evening, he was all broken up. He felt like he was diseased, different from all the other guys, and a coward in their eyes.

"That was the straw that broke the camel's back for me," the mother said. "I couldn't take it any more, so I just ran over to the parish church and cried my heart out. I said, 'God, why don't you do something? You know all the money we've spent, all the trouble we've gone through. I've done everything I can do. And now, my son is heartbroken. God, why don't you do something?'

"I heard God say, matter-of-factly, 'Why don't I do something? *You never asked me.*'

"'What do you mean, God?' I answered. 'We're praying people. We go to church. We believe in you.'"

Then she said, "In a flash, I understood what God was saying to me. Never once had I, as his mother, stopped and prayed with Johnny, expecting God's direct blessing and healing. When I thought about that, I got embarrassed and afraid. 'I've never done that,' I said to myself. `I don't know how to do it. And suppose it doesn't work? What will it do to his faith?' But, I knew I had to do it!

"I went home and found him lying in bed with his feet propped up. I walked into the room and asked, 'Johnny, do you believe that Jesus has the power to heal you?'

"He said, 'Hey, Ma, are you kidding? I pray for that every day!'

"'Yes,' I said, 'but you and I have never prayed together, asking Him, who healed the blind and the lame, to bring His healing to you right now.'

"He said, 'Well, okay!'

"So, I placed my hands on his feet, and I said a simple prayer, something like, *'Lord Jesus, You promised that wherever two or three are gathered to pray, you're there in our midst. You know and love us. You know that the doctors have not found a way to heal Johnny. Hear our prayer today. According to your will, we ask you to do what the doctors have not been able to do. Please heal my son's feet.'* We said 'Amen,' and I walked out of the room.

"In just a few days, his feet were completely cleared. He's a man now, twenty-seven years of age, and never since then has the problem come back."

I'm not saying that it always happens like that. You and I know it doesn't. Neither am I suggesting that we neglect good doctors or good medicine. God uses the things He created, and He uses people. In fact, Scripture—in the Book of Sirach, Chapter 38:1—tells us to "*hold the physician in honor.*" What I'm saying is that there is a special power in doing what Jesus taught us to do—to pray with one another—and, when hearts are open, something always happens.

For years of my life as a priest, I didn't pray that way. People would come to me with all kinds of requests, asking me to pray for them. They may have been out of work, about to have an exam, or worried about themselves or someone who was ill in their family. I'd tell them I would pray, and I meant it, but I'd often forget. Now when someone asks me, whether it's on the street, in a supermarket, at a party, on a plane, or on the telephone, I'll usually say, "Okay. You want to pray? Let's pray right now."

I remember vividly one of the first times I did this in my first pastorate on the occasion of a horrific accident. Lost for words to comfort a fellow Christian who was not Catholic, I suggested that we pray. I don't remember what I said in the prayer, but afterwards whenever I would meet this man in the community, there seemed to be a special bond between us—something that must have happened in that prayer. Since then, I've experienced over and over the effectiveness of praying with others.

When I say it's effective, I don't mean that God immediately gives the whole answer or always answers in the way we want. It might just be the beginning of an answer. It might be only that a certain peace, a certain light, or a certain direction will come. It may simply be the experience that someone cared enough to stop and pray with us as a sign of God's closeness and love. Always, it is meant to be a fulfillment of that promise of Jesus that He would be "*where two or three are gathered*" in His name. Use opportunities to pray with one another.

Husbands and wives need to pray together, even if they don't share the same faith. (But don't bug your spouse if he or she isn't ready for that! Just suggest or invite.) It doesn't have to be a long complicated prayer. As you take your partner's hand, you could simply say something like, "Lord God, thank you for bringing us together. Thank you that we're still together in spite of all we've been through. Help us, Lord, to forgive each other. Help us to know how to talk to one another and to listen and be open to each other. Help us to know how to truly love and care for each other. Help our children, Lord, and if there is something we can do to help them, show us and use us."

I remember a man to whom I suggested such a prayer. After months had passed, he shared with me, "Hey, Father, you know what you suggested about praying with my wife? There's really power in that!" Sure, it's the power of God to which we open ourselves in prayer.

How long does it take to say a prayer like that? About a minute! If husbands and wives would just take that one minute every day, what a difference it would make! So many marriages break up—even after many years! So many are unhappy. So many experience no hope or peace in the face of seemingly insurmountable problems. Why? Often, it's because they're trying to make it on their own power instead of simply and humbly asking God to do what they can never do of themselves. If the best you can do is pray on your own, do that confidently, asking God to change your own heart. You may also place a hand on your spouse or child while asleep and pray for his/her needs and those of the family as well. They won't know what hit 'em!

As I go about giving parish missions and praying with people, one of the most common things I hear is the cry of parents (grandparents, aunts, uncles, etc.) for their loved ones who are estranged from their families or the family of the Church. On the other side of this, I also hear the many heart-warming victory stories of the conversions and reconciliations resulting from sometimes many years—as St. Monica's thirty—of persevering prayer and love. St. Francis deSales said to parents, *"Yes, talk to your children about God, but more important, talk to God about your children!"*

Family members, young and old, need to pray with one another. Even if you've never done it before, break the ice and introduce it—parents with children, children with parents, brothers and sisters with one another, and relative with relative. If parents start when their children are young, they usually love it, and will often ask—even in later years, "Mom, Dad, will you pray with me?" Friends can pray with friends, fellow workers with fellow workers, and parishioners with parishioners. When others have troubles in their lives, commiserate with them, share with them, but also ask, "Do you want to pray about this? Do you want to ask God together?" On the other hand, if they have joys in their lives, listen to them. Rejoice with them. Then you can ask, "Would you like to thank God together?" If they don't want to, don't take it personally, but if they do, you will be affording them a wonderful opportunity to experience the presence, the power, the joy, and the love of Jesus.

PRAYER GROUPS

Today in our country, outside of family prayer and formal Church gatherings, there are an amazing number of small groups of people regularly coming together to pray. It's a phenomenon more widespread than ever before in my lifetime and maybe since early Christian times. I've heard about and experienced such groups in other countries as well. God is bringing His people together in and through prayer.

My friend, Jack, owned an electrical business in New Orleans. One day, on the feast of St. Joseph, he invited me to come to his shop early in the morning and pray with his employees. What I witnessed was very moving, and it happened every workday in that shop and was continued for a time by his son after Jack's death.

After everyone showed up for work and punched the clock, they gathered together and spent the first fifteen minutes to half an hour in prayer and Scripture sharing before they went out on their trucks for the day's assignments. (What a noticeable difference that made in the attitude of those workers because of the way they started their day!) Most of them were Catholic, but some weren't. Incidentally, they were paid for that first half hour.

There are many businesses, government buildings, hospitals, and homes where people are coming together to pray. In the midst of all the troubles, problems, and bad news in our world, these are centers of light and love, power and peace.

The Catholic Charismatic Movement has been preeminently responsible for fostering prayer groups and openness to all the gifts of the Holy Spirit. This movement has deeply touched my life and the lives of countless people in our country and around the world. As in every movement, there will be those who go to extremes and do or say weird or unorthodox things; however, the charismatic renewal has matured through the years and has been sanctioned by our recent Popes and our bishops as a true work of the Holy Spirit. In 1975, Pope Paul VI addressed ten thousand members of the movement and called it "a chance for the Church," an historical moment of grace. His words remind me of Our Savior's words about a special *"time of visitation"* (Lk 19:44), which Jerusalem missed, but hopefully, we won't. John Paul II has called it "a particular gift of the Holy Spirit to the Church." Meeting with a half-million representatives of various ecclesial movements from around the world, the Pope proclaimed on the vigil of Pentecost, 1998, **"Today I would like to cry out** to all of you gathered here in St. Peter's Square and to all Christians: **open yourselves docilely to the gifts of the Spirit!** Accept gratefully and obediently the charisms which the Spirit never ceases to bestow on us! Do not forget that every charism is given for the common good, that is, for the benefit of the whole Church." That's the goal and purpose of the Catholic Charismatic Renewal.

THE LITURGY

The greatest and most important community prayers are those of the liturgy, when the Church officially calls us together as a body to pray. This type of community prayer includes the Liturgy of the Hours, which priests, deacons, and most religious orders are expected to pray every day. In recent years, many lay people have started using it as well. It is made up mostly of the Psalms and readings from Sacred Scripture, and it includes morning, evening, midday, and night prayer, and even a prayer that can be said in the middle of the night, before day-break, or anytime.

Of course, the sacraments are the highest expressions of the Church's liturgy. If Jesus promised that He would be there whenever two or three are gathered to pray in His name, how much more when we gather officially as His Church to celebrate those seven unique signs of Himself that He gave us. The sacraments not only represent His risen presence and action among us, but also effectively communicate His grace. The greatest of these, and of all community prayer, is the Mass itself.

THE MASS

The Holy Spirit has enlightened and moved the hearts of many people to desire to go to Mass every day. My mother (who died at the age of ninety-six) and my dad were among them. They passed on this example and heritage to their children. Even if I were not a priest, I would want to go to daily Mass. The thousands of Masses I've offered have not tired me of the Mass. How can you get tired of love or bored with discovery? Do a bride and groom in love ever get tired of expressing their love or does an astronaut get bored with journeys into space?

It's like the old spiritual: *"So high you can't get over it, so low, you can't get under it, so wide, you can't go around it."* **There is no limit to the mystery of God's love for us expressed and communicated in the Mass. The Mass is Jesus.** It's the Word of God and the surrender of Jesus to the Father for the salvation and sanctification of the world and for my salvation and sanctification. He gave His life for that purpose in a bloody manner on the cross, but the night before He died, He did it in an unbloody way. When He said, *"This is my body...this is my blood"* (Mt 26:26-28/Mk 14:22-24/Lk 22:19-20), He was offering Himself to the Father, ritually and sacramentally, for the good of the whole world.

HIS SACRIFICE AND OURS

An ultimate **sacrifice is not just a death but a willingness to give one's life, expressed in an external way.** This willingness is still in the heart of Him who *"has a priesthood that does not pass* *away"* and who *"lives forever to make intercession"* for us (Heb 7:24-25). It is expressed in the Mass as Jesus expressed it in the Upper Room. That Supper looked forward to Calvary and is one with it; the Mass looks back on Calvary and is also one with it. *"For as often as you eat this bread and drink this cup, you proclaim the death of the Lord until he comes"* (Cor 11:26). Through the Mass, time is suspended. He makes it possible for us to be with Him at the Supper and on Calvary!

The separate consecration is a sign of death—the sign of separation of body and blood. Under that symbol, He surrendered Himself to the Father at the Last Supper in anticipation of the bloody sacrifice of the next day. Looking back to Calvary and following His command *"Do this in remembrance of me"* (Lk 22:19), we now offer this one and same sacrifice to the Father in the way Jesus did at the supper. With that sacrifice, we join our own sacrifice: our bodies, souls, sweat, work, joys, sorrows—our lives. We put them on the altar in spirit with Him every time we go to Mass and surrender them to the Father. *"Offer your bodies as a spiritual sacrifice, holy and pleasing to God, your spiritual worship"* (Rom 12:1).

That's one reason I would not want to let a day go by without Mass. I know that I never completely *let go and let God take over*. I want to, but, even unconsciously, I know that I'm holding back in some way, and so I want to come again day after day in the hope that each day I can let go a little bit more. I offer that sacrifice for my good, the good of the Church, and the good of the whole world. It's the greatest prayer that I could ever offer. Those who cannot go to Mass that often can unite themselves with the Mass offered somewhere in the world, as foretold by the prophet Malachi, *"from the rising of the sun even to its setting"* (1:11). The Apostleship of Prayer promotes the "morning offering," with different intentions for each month recommended by the Pope, as one way of doing this. The monthly intentions could be included in the diocesan newspaper, the parish announcements or bulletin, and in the prayers of the faithful.

HIS LOVE COMMUNICATED AND CELEBRATED

I also don't want to miss even one day without that special touch of God's love and power in Holy Communion. I know that He loves me whether I go to Communion or not, but as bride and groom long to express their love, tangibly and regularly, so Jesus and His bride, the Church, seek the same. *"As the deer longs for streams of water, so my soul longs for You, O God"* (Ps 42:2). Here, too, those who cannot go daily can make a "spiritual Communion," expressing in their hearts a desire for our Eucharistic Lord and for deeper union with Him.

It is from that table of *"the bread of life"* (Jn 6:48) that He sends us out each day, in spite of our weakness and bungling, empowered to bring His love, His peace, and His truth to others. I've noticed in the convents of Mother Theresa's nuns in different parts of the world, they pray the prayer of St. Francis every day after Mass: *"Lord, make me an instrument of your peace. Where there is hatred, let me bring your love. Where there is injury, pardon; where there is doubt, faith...."* As God uses them, He can use each of us as well.

In Louisiana, we know what it means to celebrate. We're always celebrating something—the Crawfish Festival, the Jambalaya Festival, the Strawberry Festival, the Jazz Festival, Mardi Gras, sports events, and on and on. It's amazing how many of us get blown away by these celebrations and then go to Mass and sit there like bumps on a log! Many don't even bother to pick up the books when a song is announced or open their mouths to make the congregational responses. Sometimes, when I hear a baby cry in church and the mother or father starts to take the child out, I'll stop (even in the middle of a sermon) and say, "Hey, don't take that child out. That baby is the only one out there showing any sign of life!"

What are we celebrating at Mass? It's the greatest reality in the world! We're celebrating the mystery that *"God so loved the world that He gave His only begotten Son"* (Jn 3:16), and that the Son so loved us that He gave Himself for our salvation. Because of that love, you and I can live a new life now and live in the fullness of life forever! Now, if that's not something to get excited about and to sing about, I don't know what there is in this whole world of ours to celebrate!

GIVE IT ALL YOU'VE GOT

In its Constitution on the Liturgy, the Second Vatican Council reminds us that *"Full and active participation by all the people...is the primary and indispensable source from which the faithful are to derive the true Christian spirit"* (#14). The world's bishops also say, *"The liturgy is the summit towards which the activity of the Church is directed; at the same time, it is the fountain from which all her power flows"* (#10). When people complain, "I'm bored at Mass," or "I didn't get anything out of it," I'd like to say, "Wow! You'd be bored to death on a date with the most wonderful person in the world if you never talked, listened, or paid any attention to that person. You'd be bored to death at a dance if you never even tapped your feet to the music."

It's a community prayer—not just a private meeting with the Lord. When a song is sung, pick up the book, read the words, and make some sound. It's a prayer, not a concert. Someone said, *"That's the only place they let me sing."* Even where we sit at Mass should express its purpose—to draw us **ever closer to God and to each other**. *"Because the loaf of bread is one, we, though many, are one body, for we all partake of the one loaf"* (1 Cor 10:17). Don't always choose the last pew or hide behind a post! Come up as close as possible to the altar and to one another.

The first question about the Mass is not "What did I get *out* of it?" but "What did I put *into* it?" We're there to give, not just to get—and we get in proportion to our giving. How much did I pray, sing, join in the responses, listen, or open and offer myself to God? The Mass is the supreme act of self-forgetful worship of the Almighty. Jesus Christ is unfailingly present and active in the Mass. He speaks to us through His Word, meets us in our praying together, ministers to us in His priest, and especially and uniquely comes to us—body and blood, soul and divinity—under the form of bread and wine.

How much do I strive to deepen my relationship with Him,

The Prayer That Pierces The Clouds And Hearts

listen to Him, communicate with Him, and join myself with Him in His surrender to the Father? No one else can do that for me. I get out of the Mass as much as I put into it. In Mark's Gospel, we read about the poor widow who gave *"all she had"* (12:44). At each Mass, I have a chance to put in more and more until, like that poor widow, it can be said of me that I gave all I had.

Especially on Sunday, *"the first day of the week,"* Christians have gathered since Apostolic times *"to break bread"* (Acts 20:7)—an expression they used for the Mass. The Council of Jerusalem clarified under the leadership of Peter that the Jewish ceremonial laws had served their purpose—leading them to Christ (Acts 15:1-29). Since they were no longer in effect, the day of His resurrection replaced the old sabbath observance.

Do you go to Mass just to fulfill that Church law and serious obligation of regular public community worship on *"the first day of the week"*? Sure, that's a good reason, but beyond that, *are you excited about going to Mass*? Suppose you lived in Jerusalem when Jesus was on earth. One day under your door you would find an invitation which read, "The Master invites you to a supper with Him the night before he lays down His life for you." Would you be touched? Would you put aside everything else and go?

The Mass is not entertainment; it's not a rock concert or a psychedelic performance and at times we priests are the ones who don't express or generate much enthusiasm. Without the eyes of faith, the Mass could be a meaningless bore for you. With faith, however, every true Mass could be the most exciting, rewarding, and moving experience of our lives. Hopefully, one day when we emerge from Mass, people would find us so happy and transformed that they would say, "I wonder what went on in there?" and they would want to come and find out.

A PRAYER ABOUT PRAYER

Lord Jesus, I ask that you teach me to pray. Teach me about prayer, but, more important, send your Spirit that I might be willing to pray and persevere in prayer, even when it seems so dry that I feel like nothing is happening. Help me to pray, not just from my

Love's the Message that I Heard

lips, but from my heart. Open my heart to all that you want to do and all that you want to say. And Mary, Mother of Jesus, great Woman of Prayer, and my spiritual Mother, pray for me.

> Lovely Lady dressed in blue,
> Teach me how to pray.
> God was just your little boy,
> And you know the way.

Our Lady of the Millennium

CHAPTER 4

The Gift Of His Church

Your part today in the mission of Jesus

"Go, therefore, and make disciples of all nations, baptizing them in the name of the Father, and of the Son, and of the Holy Spirit, teaching them to observe all that I have commanded you. And behold, I am with you always until the end of the age" (Mt 28:19-20).

Lord Jesus, guide us by your Holy Spirit to appreciate the mystery of the Church to which you have called us.

Part I
Why the Church and what is my mission in her?

WHY DO WE NEED THE CHURCH?

To begin with, why do we need the Church at all? How many people say, "I'm a good person. I don't harm anybody. I pray. I even read the Bible sometimes, but I don't need to be at worship every Sunday, listen to the Church, or be involved in it. It's just between me and God. Anyway, I don't believe in institutionalized religion."

Sound familiar? Well, what about it? Are those who say this kind of thing expressing just what **they** have to say about it or what **God** has to say? Are they following Jesus the way **He** wants to be followed or the way **they** want?

Jesus knew that He would not be visibly with us always, but He wanted His mission to continue. He therefore laid the foundation for His Church. Carefully, He chose twelve men from among His followers and especially instructed, empowered, and commissioned them for the task of leadership in His Church. It was to them that He spoke His last words on this earth: *"Go, therefore, and make disciples of all nations, baptizing...teaching..."* (Mt 28:19-20). God's plan of salvation in Jesus Christ includes the Church. It didn't stop with Jesus' earthly ministry. That's only the beginning of the story. "The rest of the story" (a la Paul Harvey) is what Jesus continues to do and teach through His body, the Church.

St. Luke clearly expresses this. After he completed his Gospel about the Lord Jesus and all He *"did and taught until the day he was taken up"* (Acts 1:1-2), he sat down and wrote the Acts of the Apostles, an account of the continued mission of Jesus through His Church. Essentially, the Church is the extension in time—through a visible sign and instrument—of the very presence and ministry of Jesus Christ among us. To reject or ignore the Church is to reject or ignore Him. *"Whoever listens to you listens to me. Whoever rejects you rejects me"* (Lk 10:16).

EXPRESSING THE MYSTERY

The Church is a mystery, like the Trinity, the Holy Eucharist, the Incarnation, and other truths revealed to us by God. To better understand what we can about a mystery, we often use earthly images, comparing it to things we understand. There are many images of the Church in Scripture. One is the image of a **sheepfold with its shepherd**, found, for example, both in the tenth and the last chapters of John's Gospel. Jesus is the great and *"good shepherd* (who) *lays down His life for the sheep"* (Jn 10:11). Before He leaves us in His visible presence, He appoints other shepherds to care for the flock in His name and with His authority. Chief among them is Peter, to whom He says, *"Feed my lambs," "Tend my sheep," "Feed my sheep"* (Jn 21:15-17).

Another is the image of **bridegroom and bride** (Eph 5:23-32). Like the above, this image also has roots in the Old Testament. Jesus is the bridegroom, and the Church, His bride.

There is also the image of the Church as a **building** made up of *"living stones"* (1 Peter 2:5-6). Jesus is the cornerstone, but He willed that there would always be in this life a visible central stone to which all the others are meant to be connected, like the cornerstone of any earthly building. He designated Peter and his succes-

The Gift Of His Church

sors as that stone, changing his name to Rock and telling him that *"...upon this rock, I will build my Church"* (Matt 16:18).

Based on the Gospel scenes of Jesus using and teaching from Peter's boat (Luke 5:3), the Church is also called "**the bark of St. Peter.**"

Finally, the image that is especially dear to St. Paul (and my favorite, too) is the image of the Church as the **body of Christ** (e.g. 1 Cor 12:12-27). As a body is made up of many members and countless body cells, so all those baptized into Christ—though spread throughout the world—form a single body, with Christ as their invisible head and the Holy Spirit as their soul.

SPOTS, WRINKLES, & SCANDALS

"Those are beautiful images," some say, "but what about the corruption in the Church? Look at the scandals, the sins, and the weaknesses! How can this be His Church or His instrument of salvation?" Well, whoever said the Church was going to be perfect and sinless in her members? She's "a refuge of sinners" all called to be saints. She's not a Church of angels but of us poor mortal men and women—good and bad, saints and sinners and in-between, glorious in some things, and sorry-looking in others.

Consider those first apostles of Jesus, His hand-picked leaders. What an unpromising bunch they often seemed to be—-so slow to understand and act! *"Do you still not understand?"* Jesus groaned (Mk 8:21). One of them betrayed Him. *"They all left him and fled"* (Mk 14:50) the night He was arrested. Three times, Peter denied he even knew Him (Jn 18:15-27). Even after His resurrection, Thomas said he wouldn't believe until he had seen with his own eyes and put his finger in the place of the nails and his hand into His side (Jn 20:25). During those forty days when He was among them again, they were still thinking politically and asking, *"Lord, are you at this time going to restore the kingdom to Israel?"* (Acts 1:6). Because of a disagreement, Barnabas and Paul had to split from one another in their mission (Acts 15:36-41). Even Peter and Paul had it out (Gal 2:11-15).

If we see the feet of clay, the spots and wrinkles (Eph 5:27) even among His own original hand-picked leaders, why should we be surprised or scandalized when we find them in the life of the Church, past and present? The history of the Church is like the story of most of us sinners—darkness and light, gloom and glory.

Some years ago in an airport between flights, I had an interesting conversation with a man from Latin America who was a writer. He made an amusing but insightful observation: "When I meet people who criticize the Catholic Church, I like to say, 'Hey, if you had a history of two thousand years, you'd have a few skeletons in your closet, too!'"

Yes, our history as Roman Catholics is none other than one of two thousand years. No reputable encyclopedia or history book would ever say anything different. There is absolutely no other beginning for the Catholic Church than with Jesus, Peter, and the apostles. In the New Testament—the Gospels, the Epistles, and the Acts of the Apostles—our roots are clearly recorded for all time.

Other Christian denominations will claim the same, but they have to admit that, somewhere along the line in those two thousand years, there were breaks from the Mother Church, and their origin is connected with that. The big break took place fifteen hundred years after Jesus, with Luther, Zwingli, Calvin, and the birth of Protestantism. Once that break took place, separated from the constant understanding, authority, and guidance of the Church and relying solely on the Scriptures, the inevitable took place. Beginning in Luther's time, Protestants began to break up among themselves—resulting in thousands upon thousands of different denominations in the course of time. As of April, 2001, the number was 33,820, with new ones being formed possibly even while you're reading this. They use the same Bible, but they disagree about its meaning.

That's not the way Jesus intended it to be. He left us a Church, guided by His Spirit, to lead us into all truth. He commissioned that Church under the leadership of Peter and the Apostles to bring His message of life to the ends of the earth. He promised, *"I am with you always"* (Mt 28:20), *"As the Father has sent me, so I send you"* (Jn 20:21), and *"Whoever listens to you listens to me"* (Lk

The Gift Of His Church

10:16). Only when we get back to listening to the Church He founded will we return to the unity that God wants for His people in this world.

Yes, in the two thousand year history of the Church, there are many things about which we are not proud. There are likewise things that happen in the Church today that provoke deep hurt, shame, and pain. We leaders—as in every family—need to seek forgiveness, reparation, and continued conversion and renewal.

Nonetheless, what we say in faith is this: in those two thousand years, Jesus Christ has never left His Church. He's never gone back on His promise, *"I am with you always, until the end of the age"* (Mt 28:20). Jesus Christ, the Captain of "the bark of St. Peter," has never abandoned ship, no matter how violently the storms have raged. Jesus Christ, the great Shepherd of His flock, has never run away when the wolves have come. Jesus Christ, the Bridegroom of His bride the Church, has never once been unfaithful to that bride. Jesus Christ, the Head of His body, has never, for one instant, separated Himself from His body.

In those two thousand years, whenever the Church has found it necessary to stand up in the world and speak—through its Council of Bishops or visible head—a clear and final word about what God wants us to do and believe on the way to eternal life, it was Jesus speaking through His Church. Whenever that Church offers us those sacraments of salvation (e.g. the forgiveness of sins, the anointing of the sick, the feeding of the flock with His very Body and Blood), it is Jesus who is ministering His love and grace to us through those visible signs. No matter who the priest is (as long as he wants to do what Jesus and His Church want and the recipient places no obstacle), it is Jesus who—faithfully, unfailingly, and without a doubt—baptizes, forgives, anoints, and feeds us with His very Body and Blood.

He worked among us through His physical body. He taught. He fed the crowds. He healed the sick. He reached out with forgiveness to sinners. He continues that work in the world now through His body, the Church. The Church is the continuation in history of the very ministry of Jesus—teaching, sanctifying, uniting, and serving the world.

Concentrating on St. Paul's image of the Church as the body of Christ, we'll zero in on three essential elements. A body has a head; a body has members; a body has to be together.

THE BODY'S HEAD

Who is Head of this body which is the Church? Our Lord, Jesus Christ, of course—but, because the body is in this world, it also needs a visible head. That's the role of the successor of St. Peter. Since nobody in his right mind even claims to be that successor (other than the Pope in Rome), it's not hard to identify the visible head of the Church.

I don't know why people have a problem recognizing the need for the Pope. What is the first thing we all do whenever we start a movement or organization and want it to go on long after we're dead? Whether it's a card club, a parish council, a school, or a government, we choose somebody as leader or head. Why do we do that? Because we know it's necessary for unity and for continuity.

Jesus knew that, and so it was the most natural thing in the world for him to choose one among the apostles to be their leader. From the Scriptures (as well as history and Sacred Tradition), it's clear that that one was Peter. Jesus said to Peter, *"To you I give the keys to the Kingdom of heaven"* (Mt 16:19). That doesn't mean that Peter's up there opening the gate to let people in! The giving of the keys was symbolic.

In those days, cities were built with a wall around them for protection. Whoever had the keys to the city was the ruler of the city. When Jesus gave Peter the keys to His kingdom, He was talking about His kingdom on earth, because He adds, *"Whatever you bind on earth shall be bound in heaven. Whatever you loose on earth, shall be loosed in heaven"* (Mt 16:19). To Peter, He is giving spiritual authority in His kingdom on earth, and the early Church recognized that.

Peter's name is mentioned in the Scriptures no less than 182 times. Second runner-up for frequent mention among the apostles is John; he's named 34 times! Some difference, eh? Peter is al-

The Gift Of His Church

ways named first in the listing of the twelve. From the beginning, Christians looked to and followed him as their leader. In the very first chapter of the Acts of the Apostles—the story of what happened after Jesus' Ascension into heaven—it was Peter who "*stood up in the midst of the brothers*" and called for the election of someone to replace the "*ministry*" or "*bishopric*" (in the original King James translation) of Judas (vv 15-28). In the next chapter, on the day of Pentecost, it's again "*Peter* (who) *stood up with the eleven*" boldly proclaiming Jesus as "*Lord and Messiah*" (vv 14 & 36) and inaugurating the mission of His Church.

There is much more that could be said about Peter's role, as given him by Jesus, from such Scripture texts as Mt 16:13-19, Jn 21:15-17, and Lk 22:31-32. What many don't know is that the Holy Spirit has been bringing more and more Protestant biblical scholars to affirm with Catholics that Peter was truly appointed by Jesus as leader of His Church and its rock-like foundation. In spite of this, what non-Catholics don't admit is that Peter's role was meant to be passed on to others in the Church—but why not? If the work of the Church is to go on—baptizing, celebrating the Lord's supper, ordaining Church leaders, teaching, and preaching—why not the role of Peter? Clearly, the first Christians recognized the need to choose someone to replace Judas, quoting the words, "... '*may another take his office*'" (Acts 1:20). Why not the office of Peter?

After Peter died, there had to be someone to take his place. Peter died in Rome and was buried there. Today, visitors can actually go down far underground to a first century street and see his tomb. It was over this spot that the huge church of St. Peter was built. Because Peter died in Rome, the Bishop of Rome came to be recognized as the central and leading Bishop of the universal Church.

The word "Pope" comes from "papa." St. Paul calls himself spiritually a "*father*" (1 Cor 4:15; 1 Thes 2:11). God's plan is for the family at home and the world-wide family of His Church also to have a papa. To be fully in union with the family is to recognize and be united with the Papa as well.

Since the Church is the Body of Christ, however, *Christ re-*

mains the invisible head of that body. The Mass is an example of what that means. At every hour somewhere in the world, a priest is taking bread into his hands at the Consecration of the Mass and saying the words of Jesus, *"This is my body."* Why does he say that? It's not the **priest's** body. He's using the Master's very words as He instructed the apostles, His first priests, to do. **Jesus, who is as intimately connected with his Body, the Church, as my head is to my body,** is, at that moment, speaking and acting through the priest. Jesus is using him to do what He Himself did in the supper room in Jerusalem two thousand years ago.

It is also the same Jesus in the Sacrament of Reconciliation who is forgiving through the words of the priest and acting and imparting His grace in all the sacraments. *Jesus Christ, the invisible Head, continues to guide and minister to us through His visible body, the Church.*

A BODY NEEDS MEMBERS

The individual human body functions through its brain and heart, its hands and feet, and millions of other body cells. What would the body of the Church be without its members? If you spelled Church "Ch__ch," what's missing? U R. You—the baptized—are the Church, together with the bishops, priests, and deacons, as servant-leaders for the body. In his famous analogy of the Church as a body, St. Paul emphasizes several times the crucial role of every member and how those who seem least important could be the most important (1 Cor 12:18-26).

Sometimes in my imagination, I picture myself sitting by Lake Galilee (or closer to home—Lake Pontchartrain), and Jesus comes along and says, "Bob, I want you." Wouldn't that be wonderful? Then I would know for sure He wants me to be ministering in His name, and He'd be backing me up every step of the way.

Well, that really happened (though not exactly that way)! It happened to me and it happened to you if you were baptized. The day the waters of Baptism flowed over our heads, Jesus was reaching out to us, calling each of us by name, and saying, "I want you." The day the bishop put his hands on me at Our Lady of Lourdes

The Gift Of His Church

Church and anointed me with the oil of Confirmation, Jesus was saying, "I'm calling you as I called Peter, James, and John to go out and continue My mission." Priestly ordination was again His call and empowerment for special service.

You might be thinking, "Man, you've got a wild imagination!" No, that's not just imagination. Do you think it was just an accident that you were baptized into His Church? Was it just an accident that you were confirmed? No, that was God's plan for you. God was calling you and He's counting on you. As He used those first disciples and those twelve apostle leaders, He wants to use you. Every day, you and I need to say with the prophet Isaiah, *"Here I am. Send me"* (Is 6:8) or with Mary *"Behold, I am the handmaid of the Lord"* (Lk 1:38).

OUR MISSION AS MEMBERS OF THE BODY

How does God use you? One way is as a member of your particular parish. Around the world, the Church is organized into dioceses and over every diocese is a bishop. Each diocese is further divided into parishes, and each parish has its own pastor. The work and worship of the universal Church is meant to come alive in each parish under the guidance of bishop and pastor, and every one of us is asked to be involved in it in some way. The mission of teaching, sanctifying, forming community, and reaching out to others in Christian service becomes our mission—the mission of every parishioner.

Are you involved in your parish, or do you sit back and expect others to do it? What happens in many parishes is that only a small percentage of people really get involved. The rest just go to church, put something in the collection basket, and think they've done their whole duty (pray, pay, and obey). It's more than that. If you're a member of that body, the Church, you've been called to be part of a great mission and to pull your share of the load. While you can't do everything, choose to do something, unless your job or family duties prevent it. It may be to work with youth or the poor, visit the sick, help with religious education, lector at Mass, or become involved with the Respect for Life Movement. If you don't know

93

what to do, go to your pastor or one of your parish leaders and ask, "How can I serve?" There is probably a task for you. Even if you're sick and housebound or bed-ridden, you may be able to use the phone, E-mail, write letters, or make rosaries. You can also offer your suffering, impairment, and confinement (or imprisonment) together with prayer for the good of the Church and the world. With St. Paul, you can say, *"Now, I rejoice in my sufferings for your sake, and in my flesh I am filling up what is lacking in the sufferings of Christ on behalf of his body, which is the church..."* (Col 1:24). Those are mysterious words but express the truth that, even though the sufferings of Jesus were more than sufficient for our salvation, we still need to join our cross with His and surrender it all to the Father for our good, the good of the Church, and of the whole world. In my parish and mission work, I have often met those who heroically do this; they are among the most powerful contributors to the work of His Church.

EVANGELIZATION

A priest friend, who revels in shockers to get people to listen (something like Jesus did), tells the parable of the grease factory. Representatives of the factory ceremoniously gave a visitor the grand tour. They explained the entire process for making grease and let him examine all the machinery.

Finally, when the tour was over and they were about to bid him farewell, the visitor asked the plant manager, "But where's your shipping department?"

"We don't have any," came the answer.

"You don't have any!" blurted out the visitor.

"No," the manager responded, "we just make enough grease to keep the machines going to make grease."

The parable says something about what we're often doing in our parishes: just keeping the plant running. We take care of the daily business and sometimes minister over and over to the same people, but what about our shipping department? What are we doing to get the message out to the neighborhood, the community, and the world that needs Jesus and His Church so badly?

The Gift Of His Church

We belong to a missionary Church—one commissioned by Christ to *"make disciples of all nations"* (Matt 28:19). *"Put out into deep water and lower your nets for a catch"* (Lk 5:4). Those words of St. Luke's Gospel were the theme of Pope John Paul's apostolic letter, *At the Beginning of the New Millennium,* calling us to a new depth of holiness (*"into deep water"*) and again to the "New Evangelization" (*"for a catch"*). Paul VI, the Pope shortly before him, in *Evangelization in the Modern World #14*, had challenged us with the message: the Church "exists to evangelize." If you are the Church—**you exist to evangelize.**

As members of His Church, God calls each of us to share with others all that He shares with us, and that means especially sharing our Faith—the most precious gift He has given us. It is amazing how many Christians are not conscious of this mission and the opportunities that are theirs. Some who are reading this have gone to church for many years, have heard sermon after sermon, may have attended retreats, cursillos, or special programs of instruction and renewal, or have read and studied on their own. Why did God in His goodness and providence give you these opportunities? Was it simply to keep for yourself, or was it to share with others—those who have very little or nothing of all this or those who regrettably have lost what they had?

The first time you meet somebody, you don't have to share the whole Gospel right off the bat. That's one reason why Jesus chose fishermen as his apostles. A fisherman learns how to wait as he patiently lures the fish. He gets a nibble, then a bite, and only then, hooks the fish and hauls it in. So, normally, you don't go up to a stranger and immediately start talking about Jesus and His Church. Introduce yourself. Get acquainted. Become a friend. As they say in the Cursillo movement, "Make a friend; then, bring a friend to Christ."

One day in my mother's later years, I called her on the phone and asked how she was doing.

"Oh! I'm feeling so bad," she said, "I can hardly pray! All I can do is say 'Jesus'."

"Hey Ma," I answered, "that's a good prayer. Just say 'Jesus'."

I never thought it meant that much to my mother, but, some

Love's the Message that I Heard

years after she died, I got a call from a hospital chaplain. He told me that there was a man in intensive care who said that, one day, he was doing some work for my mother, and she shared this incident with him. He remembered it in the ICU and, hopefully, was calling on the name of Jesus.

It was a very simple thing that I said to my mother, but it touched her, helped her, and she passed it on. How many times have we been enlightened about something or touched by God's grace in some way? God gave that to you not to hoard just for yourself but as a gift and treasure to share with your brothers and sisters along the way. That's what it means to share *"your testimony"* or to *"witness"* (2 Tim 1:8, Acts 1:8). It's one of the most effective ways to evangelize. Whatever you can do or say to help open someone's heart wider to Jesus Christ, His Gospel, or His Church—do it; say it.

I conducted a parish mission in Mobile, Alabama some years ago. Afterwards, a man wrote me something like this:

"There was a man in my neighborhood (we'll call him Joe) who was a veteran and an invalid. His wife and children were Catholic, but he didn't belong to any denomination. I used to visit him from time to time. After the mission, I had the courage to do something that otherwise I might not have done. I went to visit him, and, after we talked for awhile, I said, 'Joe, did you ever think about becoming a member of the Church?' He said, 'Aw no, I'm not interested.' So, I didn't push it, but before I left, I asked him if he'd like to say a prayer with me.

He said, 'Okay,' so we just prayed one Our Father together. After the prayer, I said, 'Joe, your family has been brought up Catholic, and maybe at times you've wondered why they do the things they do and believe what they believe. Suppose I invite the parish priest to stop by and visit you? You could ask him questions and talk to him about some of the things that may have come to mind over the years.'

'Well, all right,' he said. So I got a priest, and a series of conversations began between him and my friend. Joe was eventually baptized and received the Body and Blood of Christ for the first time. Shortly after that, he got very ill, and God took him home."

The Gift Of His Church

The man wrote me of the tremendous consolation and joy at Joe's funeral, especially in the heart of his wife, because, before he died, he came to Christ and His Church. God used that friend to be His instrument in bringing another man to Him—not by pushing, but by loving, inviting, waiting, and praying. It's worth noting that it was the prayer together that seemed to open Joe's heart and give his friend the words to say to him. Prayer is such a simple yet powerful reality that we can share with others in many different circumstances.

There's a world out there. There are countless persons who have separated themselves from the Lord and from His Church and others who have never been his disciples. Among them are untold numbers who are restless and searching and whose interest could be awakened. With the lame man in John's gospel, they might say, "*I have no one...*" (5:7). They need another to reach out to them.

If you are a Catholic Christian, God has given you a great gift and treasure (Mt 13:44)—the treasure of faith in Him in His Church. Every day is a chance to learn more about Our Lord, the Scriptures, and the Church. Take time for reading, studying, and listening to cassettes, etc., so that, as St. Peter says, you can "*always be ready to give an explanation to anyone who asks you for a reason for your hope*" (1 Pt 3:15). Not all will welcome or search out a priest for the many questions that trouble them, but they will often use an opportunity to talk with someone else who seems interested and able to enlighten them. You might not have all the answers, but you can share something with them, offer to pray with them, give them or refer them to something to read or someone else who might help them.

1-800-My Faith, with the approval of many bishops, is available Monday through Friday to answer questions about Catholicism. The caller will speak person to person and will usually receive, as a follow-up, something written—brief and to-the-point—on the subject at hand. The organization called Catholic Answers has a similar service and much literature, brief tracts, two publications, a call-in program, and some cassettes as well (1-888-291-8000 or www.Catholic.com).

Love's the Message that I Heard

St. Joseph Communications (1-800-526-2151) has produced thousands of cassettes (with some videos and CD's) on various aspects of the Faith. Conveniently, these can be listened to while dressing, working around the house, jogging, or going to work. Call for their free catalogue. Conversion cassettes are especially inspiring and instructive. Over 400 Protestant ministers in the U.S. have become Catholic in recent years, assisted greatly by The Coming Home Network (1-800-664-5110). The Network sponsors "The Journey Home" convert program on international EWTN/T.V. (and their radio network). EWTN carries a host of other enlightening and moving programs twenty-four hours a day (205-271-2900). They will also advise callers inquiring about how to get the programming into their area.

On the last day, when you and I stand in judgment, He's not *just* going to ask, "Did you commit adultery? Did you miss Mass?" He's also going to ask, "What did you do with the treasure that I gave you? Did you just keep it *"buried...in the ground"* (Mt 25:25-30)? How much did you share it with others?"

BEING WITNESSES

Finally, God wants to use you to be an example, a witness, and an instrument of His work and His kingdom right where you are— in marriage and family life, single or divorced, in the neighborhood or at work, in business and education, and in medicine, politics and recreation. There's a little ditty: *"Mr. Business went to church and never missed a Sunday. Mr. Business went to hell for what he did on Monday!"* Monday, Tuesday, Thursday—all are God's days, and everything we do is His business. Yes, go to church, especially to the Holy Eucharist. That's the primary source of the grace, strength, and guidance we need, but bring all that with you when you leave the church and put it into practice in your daily life. Every aspect of life is meant to be renewed by the presence and action of Christians involved in it. Evangelization is not just one on one but the radical transformation of modern culture and ways of life. That's lay persons' special role—beginning with the family.

The Gift Of His Church

My mother belonged to one of the old elite social clubs in New Orleans. In her advanced years, she sat down and wrote a letter to the president of the club inquiring if it were open to all races. My mother prayed the rosary and attended Mass every day until she was no longer able. She had come to realize, however, that to be a Christian also meant to be a Christian in her social life and in the organizations she supported.

My dad had a great consciousness of community responsibility. He told me that, when people asked him to be on committees of various kinds, they often ended up regretting it. The reason was that, as a man of integrity and moral conviction, he spoke his own mind regardless of popularity or political correctness.

I have a friend who has a printing business along Bayou Lafourche. It's called "Master's Prints". I asked him one day why he called it that. "Do you think you're the 'master' of all the printers?"

"No," he said, "but I've handed my business over to the Master. That's why I've given it that name."

Years ago, not long before Christmas, I gave a mission in Pine Prairie, Louisiana. (In case you don't know where Pine Prairie is, it's right next to Turkey Creek!) When the mission was over, the pastor suggested that, on my way out of town, I stop by to meet the local pharmacist. It was night, and he and his wife were alone in the store, just closing up. He told me a very simple but moving story. "A few weeks ago on the Feast of Christ the King, I was at Mass," he said, "and I could hear Jesus ask me in my heart, 'Tommy, am I your King?' And I said, 'Sure, Lord, you're my King.' Then I could hear Him ask, 'Am I the King of everything?' That's when I knew I had to do it—something I'd been struggling with. That night, I went into my pharmacy and wrote a letter to my customers. I told them that, in this pharmacy, I would no longer be selling contraceptives, including the pills. I had decided to let Jesus Christ be Lord and King of my Pine Prairie pharmacy." God blessed him. Tommy was doing very well in his business and was a truly happy man. He was a witness.

The world needs witnesses, young and old—living testimonies of what it means to be followers of Christ. What would restaurants, medical, or political offices—every business and institution—look like and be like if Jesus were the boss? That's the Christian's challenge. Gandhi of India is reported to have said, "If the Christians would live their lives according to the teachings of Jesus Christ, there would be no Hindus left in India!"

Part II
A Body has to be together.

Unity and Reconciliation

"The Church is herself the great sacrament of Christ, a sign and instrument of communion with God and of unity among all" (Vatican Council II, Dogmatic Constitution on the Church #1).

A body has to be together. Take your own body, for example. Suppose one hand wants to go in one direction, and the other disagrees. Suppose one foot wants to go in one direction and the other in the opposite direction. What would happen? You wouldn't go anywhere except on your derriere! On this side of heaven, that's what happens so often in the body that is the Church. Not only are there many thousands of different Christian denominations disagreeing among themselves but also divisive factions among members of the one Catholic Church, herself.

In John's Gospel, at the Last Supper on the night before He died, Jesus cries out from the depth of His heart: *"I pray not only for them, but also for those who will believe in me through their word, so that they may all be one, as you, Father, are in me and I in you, that they also may be in us,* **that the world may believe that you sent me.** *And I have given them the glory you gave me, so that they may be one, as we are one"* (John 17:20-22).

That's the great sign the world needs and the sign by which He said it would believe. When we start coming together in unity, the world will say, "Now, that's a miracle! Only God could bring that about!" On the other hand, our disunity as Christians and as Catholics is a blatant scandal! "If they can't get along and agree

The Gift Of His Church

even among themselves," outsiders say, "why should we bother?" More than any other denomination, the Catholic Church has the basic elements and structure for unity: visible Leadership, common universal worship especially in the Mass and seven sacraments, and a clear code of doctrine and law, but we have a long way to go to give the witness of unity that the world needs and for which Jesus prayed. What would it be like, for example, if all of us who call ourselves Catholic would come together on **even one** moral issue, like that paramount issue of respect for human life? Suppose one day we'd all go down on our knees and cry out to God from the depths of our hearts to end the slaughter of the unborn, adding, "Lord, whatever you want us to do about it, here we are. Use us." I believe that day would mark the beginning of turning back the tide! But—we're so half-hearted, so timid, and—on many issues—so divided.

UNITY IN FAITH

The unity that we need is, first of all, a unity in faith. The early Christians were *"of one heart and mind"* (Acts 4:32). St. Peter warns against *"false teachers among you who will introduce destructive heresies"* and lead many from *"the way of truth"* (2 Pt 2: 1-2). From the beginning, the Church had the commission from Jesus to teach the life-giving truth. Her creeds and catechisms throughout history were to ensure clarity and unity in her teachings. In recent years (1993), the official Catechism of the Catholic Church (which, together with the Bible, every Catholic home should have) has again proclaimed them with deeper insights for our day. Ask a cross-section of Catholics today, however, what they believe about important matters of faith, such as "What happens when we die?" or "Is Christ really present in the Eucharist?" and you'll get all kinds of different answers.

Sure they believe in heaven, but how many believe in hell? Well, the same Jesus who offers us the gift of eternal life taught us that we can freely and eternally forfeit that gift. As for purgatory, it's often just ignored. Praying for the dead, however, was a regular practice of God's people in both Old and New Testament times.

Scripture and Tradition approvingly witness to this (2 Mac. 12:38-46, 2 Tim. 1:18). If prayer is not needed by those in heaven, and it's useless for those in hell, then who else could we be praying for when we pray for the dead except for those in purgatory?

Belief in the Real Presence of Christ in the Eucharist is another source of division within our Church. Many Catholics, even some who go to church regularly, consider the Holy Eucharist as just a symbol, just a reminder. On the other hand, the Church from the beginning has taken Jesus' words to heart. (Mt 26:26-28/Mk 14:22-24/Lk 22:19-20/Jn 6:27-71/1Cor 11:23-30.) She has consistently believed, taught, and practiced that this is really the Body and Blood of Our Lord Jesus Christ, mysteriously but truly present under the form of bread and wine.

UNITY AND MORALITY

When it comes to moral issues, there is even more public disagreement among Catholics. Morality has an impact on every aspect of life—business, medicine, politics, economics, recreation, and international relations. The news media, however, usually zero in on sexual morality in highlighting divisions among Catholics. They ask questions like how many believe that premarital sex, homosexual practices, or artificial birth control is wrong? It's amazing how many Catholics will say they believe these things are all right.

Well, how do we know what is right and wrong regarding all these issues? Do we just keep taking polls to find out what the majority has to say? If we did that, we'd be in a mess—which is where so many are. Morality changes for them with the winds of public opinion or personal sentiment, with what's politically correct, or even what's legally permitted.

Is that the way Jesus chose to guide us down through the ages? He came as *"...the light of the world"* (Jn 8:12). Did the Light go away and leave us in the dark? What did He say when He was about to take His leave? Was it "every man for himself" or "may the majority win" ? No, He **gave us a Church** under the guidance of Peter and the apostles and their successors, solemnly commis-

The Gift Of His Church

sioning them, *"Go...make disciples of all nations...teaching them"* **with authority in His name.** He promised, *"I am with you always"* **in that mission** *"until the end of the age"* (e.g. Mt 28:16-20). He did not just abandon the bark of Peter to the wind and waves of political correctness and popular sentiment. He's the ever-faithful, though unseen, captain who pledged to steer the ship of His Church always 'til the end and by *"the Spirit of truth...**guide you to all truth**"* (Jn 16:12). In every age, the Church's mission, guided by the Holy Spirit, is to apply the teachings of Jesus to the questions and challenges of the day. As Vatican Council II expressed this in modern times: "**In the formation of their consciences, the Christian faithful ought carefully to attend to the sacred and certain doctrine of the Church.** The Church is, by the will of Christ, the teacher of the truth. It is her duty to give utterance to and authoritatively to teach that Truth which is Christ Himself, and also to declare and confirm by her authority those principles of the moral order which have their origin in human nature itself" (Declaration on Religious Freedom #4, emphasis added).

There was a time when I used to be impressed with what the majority had to say. Now, I often conclude that if the majority says it's right, chances are it's wrong! God's Word is *"...a sign that will be contradicted"* (Lk 2:34) always challenging us: *"Do not conform yourself to this age but be transformed by the renewal of your mind..."* (Rom 12:2)

CATHOLICS AND CONTRACEPTION

Let's say something particularly about that issue of contraception. The polls indicate that the large majority of married Catholics in their fertile years have either had themselves sterilized or are using some unnatural form of birth control. Historically, the widespread dissent from Church teaching on this issue that erupted in the late sixties decidedly led to dissent on other areas of sexual morality and even doctrinal matters. The chances are that most of the dissenters thought they were in their rights.

If couples had asked me twenty years ago about contraception (as some did), I was inclined to go along with the current thinking. In any case, I would have told them that it was up to them to make a conscientious decision, after considering everything. *Now*, I urge them with all my heart to follow the guidance of the Church and form their consciences accordingly. I'm convinced that here, *true compassion is to speak the truth compassionately.*

Many things have brought me to this point. One is a new appreciation of the urgent need for attention to the Church's teaching mission in a world that has lost a sense of any objective right or wrong or even of objective truth itself. When we *"refuse to listen even to the church"* (Mt 18:17) *"to whom shall we go?"* for *"the words of eternal life"* ((Jn 6:68). Related to this are the disastrous consequences of the "make up your own mind" or the "form your own conscience" directive. It's been used to justify everything under the sun!

Through the years, I've also learned more about Natural Family Planning, morally permissible for couples who have a serious reason to avoid or postpone another pregnancy. Modern-day NFP has been perfected as far beyond the old Rhythm Method as the auto over the buggy. It does not require a regular menstrual cycle and usually calls for only a comparatively brief time of abstinence each month. It can be 99% effective—as effective as *all* the ongoing contraceptives and more effective than some. A *British Medical Journal* article of 1993 cites a study of almost 20,000 women in India who used Natural Family Planning with practically no pregnancies among them. Almost every Catholic diocese offers courses in it.

Actually, the turning point in my own thinking began with a brilliant woman's presentation on the effectiveness and benefits of Natural Family Planning contrasted with the harmful effects—physical, psychological, and spiritual—of artificial birth control. The most alarming part of this presentation alerted me to the fact **that all the chemical contraceptives** (including all the pills, Norplant, Depo-Provera injections, and IUD's) **have a possible abortive effect.** They all allow for break-through ovulation (some more than others) and alter the lining of the uterus which "reduces the likelihood of implantation." (The quote is from the standard

The Gift Of His Church

Physician's Desk Reference regarding the action of birth control pills.) Couples having sexual relations can therefore sometimes conceive, but *interference with implantation can mean death for the one-week-old new human being.*

Though there are physicians who contest this, well over two hundred doctors have recently signed "A Declaration of Life" affirming the potentially abortive effect of all the above mentioned chemical contraceptives. (American Life League, P.O.Box 1350, Stafford, VA 22555, (540) 659-4171.) The recent contraceptive patch could also be included on the list. The World Federation of Doctors Who Defend Human Life has also circulated information regarding the abortive potential (by a different mechanism) of the spermicides which contain the chemical Nonoxonol-9 (with which some condoms are coated and often used with the female barrier methods as well).

For me, all this was like nature's warning light flashing: "Something's wrong with contraception; something's right with Natural Family Planning." It also showed me how, long before the pill, the Church's ancient teaching was prophetically safeguarding not only marriage and sex, but human life as well. The Church isn't behind the times; she's been way ahead of the times, warning us all along: "Don't mess with God's domain."

All I've said here and will say is not to put anyone unjustifiably on a guilt trip. Many have used contraceptives without any knowledge of the above, and most Catholics have never had an in-depth presentation on the issue. Many, too, have been wrongly advised by well-meaning priests like me (years ago). For the others who chose the wrong path with eyes wide-open, there is the call to conversion of mind and heart and a Father of Mercy with welcoming arms ready to embrace and forgive.

God's moral law is His loving plan for us. The violation of it is a violation of the great command to *"love the Lord, your God, with all your heart, with all your soul, and with all your mind* (and)...*love your neighbor as yourself "* (Mt 22:37 & 39). We know His law from reason and from human nature as created by God and from what He has revealed.

The main reason why contraception is wrong is because it's

human interference in an area that uniquely belongs to God and His design. Jesus was calling us back to our roots when He said, *"Have you not read that from the beginning the Creator made them male and female and said 'For this reason a man shall leave his father and mother and be joined to his wife, and the two shall become one flesh'? So they are no longer two but one flesh. Therefore, what God has joined together, no human being must separate"* (Mt 19:4-6). **God made man and woman. He made sex— we didn't invent it. It's His own wonderful work and plan of love, and it needs to be respected and exercised in the way He intended. In sharing with us the power to give life, He joined it to an intimate expression of self-giving love. To unnaturally separate the act of love from its possible life-giving effect is to tamper with and seriously violate a sacred design of God.** When nature provides non-fertile periods, it's God's work; when we create them against nature's plan in order to circumvent that plan, we act against His will.

Let me give an example. Let's say you sit down to eat a delicious meal, but before doing so, you put a tube in your throat to catch the food. You still get the taste of eating and the socializing that may go with it, but then you take the tube after you're finished and throw it in the garbage can. Sorry if it seems crude, but what's the difference between that and the use of condoms, diaphragms, foams, pills, oral or anal sex, mutual masturbation, and all the rest? All are designed—one way or the other—to block, destroy, or interfere with the natural effect of the marriage act. The pleasure of the act is achieved to an extent, but the life-giving result intended by the Creator is unnaturally frustrated. The difference between this and Natural Family Planning is that, in NFP, the couple is not **abusing** but **using** nature. They **do not interfere in the act itself, a sacred God-designed process**, but by self-control, make use of the natural rhythm of fertile and non-fertile days as designed by the Creator. To continue the eating analogy: periodically, **you can either eat or fast, but when you choose to eat, you can't deliberately block its life-giving effect**.

Another less graphic and more subtle way of looking at it is this: **Sexual intercourse is meant to express the total gift of**

The Gift Of His Church

oneself to another without anything being held back. As Vatican II puts it, the marriage act should, "by objective standards... preserve the full sense of mutual self-giving and human procreation in the context of true love" (#51—The Church in the Modern World). It is intended by God to be an expression and renewal of the couple's marriage agreement and covenant. It is God's way for them to say over and over again, "I take you and give myself to you for better or worse, for richer or poorer, in sickness and in health, without reservation, until death." **In the use of contraceptives of any kind, a couple is not saying this unreservedly. There is a hidden agenda, a holding back, a conditional consent: "I am giving myself to you but not completely."**

The marital union, modeled on the life of the Trinity and the union of Christ and His Church, is a call to total unselfish self-giving and holiness. *"Husbands, love your wives, even as Christ loved the Church and handed himself over for her to sanctify her..."* (Eph 5:25-26). **Unnaturally blocking off fertility (an integral part of who a person is) in the very act of marriage always contradicts the complete self-donation and holiness (wholeness) of the act.**

What is said above would also (and even more so) apply to the act of *permanent sterilization* for the sole purpose of birth control, carrying with it the added evil of unjustified bodily mutilation. The more than one million a year sterilizations in the United States are not without their own harmful side-effects—physical, psychological, and spiritual.

Did you know that, before 1930, all the Christian denominations were in agreement about the evil of artificial birth control? Protestant denominations (which began in the 1500's) still stood shoulder to shoulder with the Catholic Church on the subject for about four hundred years. It was in 1930 that one denomination, the Anglican bishops at their Lambeth Conference in England, made some limited exceptions regarding marital contraception. Twice before in the 1900's, the Lambeth Conference had unequivocally condemned all contraception. Why the change in 1930? Was it enlightened progress or secular conformism?

This was the beginning of a general collapse of other Christian denominations on this issue and then, for some, on other aspects of sexual morality and abortion as well. A crack had been made in the dike of clear sexual moral teaching, and the whole structure began to fall. Thank God that the Catholic Church, in spite of all the public uproar, has stood her ground *"...in the breach..."* (Ez 22:30). Especially through the voice of the successors of St. Peter, **she continues to call the world back to God's plan for man and woman, for life, for sex, and for marriage. If God is invited out of the most intimate relationship of husband and wife, their marriage begins to deteriorate and the family with it. Pope John Paul keeps reminding us that "the future of the world and of the Church passes through the family."**

There is much more that could be presented about all this, but other sources are available. In *The Gift of the Church,* a Queenship Publication, I devote a whole chapter, as well as an appendix, to the subject. Strongly recommended are Dr. Janet Smith's books on this issue and her popular, brilliant, and witty cassette, *Contraception—Why Not?* (1-800-307-SOUL). That, together with John Kippley's *Marriage Is For Keeps*, is a must for couples preparing for marriage. Kippley has been the guiding spirit behind The Couple to Couple League, which promotes one of the Natural Family Planning methods (1-800-745-8252 or CCLI.org). Pope John Paul's "Theology of the Body" has been popularized by Christopher West through his book *Good News About Sex & Marriage* (Servant Publications, Ann Arbor, MI) and on his cassettes and videos (Our Father's Will Communications, 1-866-333-OFWC).

Dr. Thomas Hilgers and the staff of the Pope Paul VI Institute for the Study of Human Reproduction provide help for a variety of reproductive and fertility problems, assisting women and couples who want to abide by the moral law (Omaha: 402-390-6600). Pharmacists For Life, together with the Pope Paul VI Institute, can offer alternative remedies to the pill for various medical conditions such as endometriosis, irregularity, etc. They can also advise and support pharmacists who want to avoid dispensing objectionable drugs (1-888-872-5030).

Of course, the most celebrated and contested treatment of the subject of contraception is the encyclical of Pope Paul VI, *Humanae*

The Gift Of His Church

Vitae ("Of Human Life"), issued in 1968 during the sexual revolution. In it, he reiterates in modern terms a consistent moral teaching that goes back to early Christianity—upholding God's plan and condemning any contraceptive use of marital relations that violates the intimate, God-given connection between the unitive and procreative meaning of the act.

When I was first exposed to this encyclical, I was so influenced by the news commentators and the protesting theologians that I didn't think that much of it. Years later, when the smoke had cleared and I read it calmly, thoughtfully, and with an open mind and heart, I was deeply impressed with the profound wisdom and love it conveys. It's like the young guy who said, "You know, when I was eighteen, I thought my dad was pretty stupid. But when I got to be twenty-one, I was amazed how much he had learned in three years!"

When we have trouble accepting some solemn teaching of the Church, we shouldn't presume that she just hasn't gotten "with it" or that we have some special insight that this Church of two thousand years has not yet considered. Instead, why not presume that we're the ones who haven't yet caught up with the Church or plumbed the depth of her wisdom and insights. Make the effort to pray, to study, and, regarding a subject like contraception, to consult those theologians, doctors, and married couples who are with the Church on the issue. The witness of Natural Family Planning couples is powerful. Whereas the divorce rate for U.S. couples is alarming, a recent study shows that for those using Natural Family Planning divorce is almost nil. They often testify to the many other blessings, including the sacrifice, that accompany NFP.

TOGETHER IN LOVE

As we need to be together in His Church in faith, we also need to be together in forgiveness and love. That calls for daily grace and effort.

My Cajun friend, Msgr. Sigur, used to say, "You know what Jesus said about *'Where two or three are gathered together...'* Well, where two or three are gathered together, chere, there's trouble!"

Love's the Message that I Heard

When you get people together in the family, at work, or in the parish, eventually, somebody is going to disagree with someone else. Someone is going to hurt someone else.

It happens at home. Why should we be surprised or even scandalized when it happens in the wider family of the Church? Always remember that it's Jesus' Church, and the Holy Spirit is her soul. In that Church, there are the two great instruments of ongoing forgiveness, unity, and charity—the Sacraments of Reconciliation and of the Holy Eucharist. Because of all this, **there is more power to heal than to hurt and more power to unite than to divide.** Each reconciliation between people can result in even stronger bonds of unity and love.

One way we can heal, unite, and build up the body is by **affirmation.** Do you know what happens when you begin to get involved in the work of the Church? A lot of those who don't get involved sit back and criticize. Sound familiar? It's a game parishioners play. Don't join it. Do the opposite. If you're not ready or able to jump in and help, at least affirm and encourage those who do. Say, "Hey, Joe or Mary, I'm not ready to do what you're doing, but I certainly appreciate the fact that you've stepped forward, and I want you to know that I'm praying and pulling for you."

Encouragement and affirmation are meant to begin at home with husband and wife and family members. What happens in so many marriages is that, when a couple is courting, they work hard at being polite and "lovey-dovey". They go out of their way for one another—complimenting, overlooking faults, and bringing out the best in each other. When they're riding in a car together, they couldn't get closer. Six months after the wedding, they're hanging out of the windows on opposite sides!

What happened? They knew that they were just two human beings with faults, limitations, and potentially conflicting differences; however, they managed to overlook all that, see each other through the eyes of love, and emphasize the positive. After they've won the prize and gotten married, they relax the effort and start focusing on all the negative things. We all have them, you know, and we could pick one another to death by harping on them.

The Gift Of His Church

(My wife (husband) is an angel; she (he) is always *harping* on something!)

There is a time and place for honest talk about things that are adversely affecting our relationships and communities, but words and deeds that give encouragement and show appreciation are especially needed. Family members are called to do this for one another. What is done at home is also needed in the family of the parish, the Church, and the community at large.

What should be done when we do hurt someone or someone hurts us? Has it ever happened in your life? Is there a person alive to whom it hasn't? Forgiveness, of course, is again the answer, remembering that it's first of all a decision, and the key to it is opening our hearts to Jesus Christ and His grace.

A woman told me this simple story. "I was at Mass one day, and this other woman was also at Mass. Now I said to Jesus at Communion time, 'Lord, you know I don't like that woman. I have a hard time getting along with her, but I know You forgive her and love her, so You take over and **forgive her and love her in me and through me**.' Well, we went to breakfast afterward, and it was wonderful!"

Besides this, what did Jesus say to do if we've been hurt by someone? Yes—forgive, pray for the person, and even return good for evil, but He added something else that we often miss: "*If your brother sins (against you), tell him his fault between you and him alone. If he listens to you, you have won over your brother. If he does not listen, take one or two others along with you... if he refuses to listen to them, tell the church*" (Mt 18:15-17).

How many of us do that? You know what some of us do? We get on the telephone and tell ten other brothers and sisters what our brother or sister did. That's exactly what Jesus said not to do. "Tell **him**," the offending person—not everyone else. Unless it's something that needs to be taken care of as soon as possible, seek the right time to avoid serious harm. If you can't do it peacefully today, tomorrow, or even next month or next year because of the circumstances, forgive, pray, act charitably, and say, "Lord, I don't know when or how, but You open the door for the two of us to get together. Give me the grace to walk through that open door and to be a channel of Your peace and an instrument of Your reconciliation." Contacting the other person (even by correspondence) **does not mean attacking.** It usually means **owning and acknowledging our own concerns and feelings** without accusation, admitting that we may have possibly misunderstood or over-reacted and saying that our purpose is understanding, reconciliation, and healing.

What about those negative things we hear so often about other people. Here again we have the opportunity to respond destructively or constructively. **Destructively,** we could gloat over the bad news, rejoicing that we're not the ones being criticized. We could also add to the negative talk and even pass it on to others. **Constructively,** we could urge prayer in the situation and forgiveness (silently, or if possible, aloud, offering a prayer right then and there). We might share something good about the person criticized and suggest a meeting with the person, even offering to facilitate it. This latter would be the Christ-like response.

If we ask ourselves what Jesus actually did and what His mission was when He was among us, we might think of a number of things: teaching, sacrificing His life, opening heaven for us, instituting His Church. One word seems to get at the heart of His mission and that is "mediator." A mediator is a go-between, a connecting bridge for estranged persons. In life, there are many mediators, but for all of us together there is *"one mediator between God and the human race, Christ Jesus, himself human, who gave himself as ransom for all"* (1 Tim 2:5).

His mission was to open our way for reconciliation with the Father and with one another. The cross symbolizes this work of Jesus. On the wood of the cross, He became that "bridge over troubled water," laying Himself down to heal our broken relationship with God and with one another. The vertical beam reaching from earth to heaven symbolizes His role of uniting us with God. The horizontal beam, with arms outstretched, represents His call to all humanity for reconciliation with one another in and through Him.

Listen once again to those words of Paul to the Corinthians. *"You then are the body of Christ. Every one of you is a member of it"* (1 Cor 12:27, NAB unrevised edition). The mission of reconciliation, of being a bridge, has been passed on to us, His body, the Church. Every one of us is called to share in it. *"God...has reconciled us to himself through Christ and given us the ministry of reconciliation"* (2 Cor 5:18). By God's grace, when people encounter you, it will be Christ dwelling in you that they are meeting and through you are being brought closer to Him and to one another.

PRAYER

O God, our Father, we thank you for the amazing gift You have given us in Jesus and His Church. Help us to embrace that gift and the responsibility that goes with it. Holy Spirit, enlighten and strengthen us. Set our hearts on fire, as you set on fire the hearts of those first disciples and apostles, who went out, even to death, bringing the Good News of Jesus to the world.

St. Peter and all you "twelve apostles of the Lamb," foundation stones of the New Jerusalem (Rev 12:14), intercede for us before God's throne. Mary, as a mother, you want your spiritual children to be together "that the world may believe" (Jn 17:21) in your Son; pray for us. St. Joseph, patron of the Universal Church, you who took care of the family of Jesus and Mary, pray for the family that is God's Church.

THE SACRAMENT OF RECONCILIATION

Putting Flesh on His Forgiveness

The Church's on-going mission of reconciliation is expressed and carried out in the course of our lives through a special Sacrament called Reconciliation.

A woman once told me this story. She said, "Father, I used to go to confession, but I stopped. I would say to myself, 'I don't need to go to confession. I can just tell my sins to God.'" (How many times have you heard that one!) "Then one day when I was telling my sins to God," she said, "God told me, '*I want you to go to confession!*' God even gave me a reason. He said, 'I want you to go to confession because *I want to put flesh on My forgiveness.*'"

That's a simple and profound expression of the whole plan and mystery of salvation in Jesus Christ and His Church. **God didn't have to do it that way.** He didn't have to become one of us, take on our human nature, or die on a cross, but He wanted to make Himself and His love visible and tangible to us. When He left this earth in that visible, tangible way, He left behind a visible, tangible Church, His body, through which He continues to minister to us. In that Church, the particular sign and instrument of His forgiveness, is the Sacrament of Reconciliation.

In the Gospel, we read that, on the night of His resurrection, Jesus appears to His Apostles, who were huddled together in fear. He commissions them, *"As the Father has sent me, so I send you"* (Jn 20:21), and He empowers them particularly for the forgiveness of sins. He breathes on them—a sign of this empowerment. *"Receive the Holy Spirit. Whose sins you forgive are forgiven them, and whose sins you retain are retained"* (Jn 20:23). They and their successors will be used as signs and instruments of His forgiveness.

When we go to confession, we don't see Jesus. At Mass, we don't see Jesus either, but it is the same Jesus, through the ministry of His priest, who changes bread and wine into His Body and Blood at Mass and who forgives sins in the Sacrament of Reconciliation.

It's also the Church forgiving, because every sin that we commit, in some way, affects other people. If I hold anger, unforgiveness, pride, or lust in my heart, I can't say that it's just my own business. No, it's affecting other people. I'm connected with all my brothers and sisters in the family and body of the Church. In some way, I'm blocking the flow of God's life, love, and peace. I can't be as effective an instrument of that life to others. In fact, I'd probably contribute something negative rather than positive to them. When I repent of that, especially when it involves a serious sin, it's not sufficient for me just to tell God I'm sorry. I also need to tell my brothers and sisters that I'm sorry. I don't have to stand up on Sunday morning and tell my sins to the whole congregation. When I go to the priest, the one ordained for that ministry as brother and father in the family, and he forgives, it's as if the whole Church embraces me and says, "We forgive you, too. You're reconciled with us, your family, the Church."

The Gift Of His Church

Surprising for some, there are a lot of people outside of the Catholic Church who appreciate confession more than many Catholics. I've visited and offered Mass in prisons a good number of times. Before the service, I'll afford a time for confession. I'll explain that, if there are some who are not Catholic, I cannot give sacramental absolution. "You can still come in, however," I'll tell them, "and talk, unburden yourself, and ask for prayer." Many who are not Catholic will use that opportunity. The need to tell someone else is deep in the hearts of all human beings.

The program of AA, Alcoholics Anonymous, works successfully with people around the world of countless different denominations, and even people of no religious profession. In AA (to quote their own literature), after acknowledging dependence upon "a Power greater than ourselves" members are urged to make a "searching and fearless inventory" of themselves. The fifth step then calls for "admitting to God, to ourselves, and to *another human being* the exact nature of our wrongs."

AA knows the human condition. They know that, if we want to get our lives together, it's not sufficient just to get in touch with God but that we also need someone else with whom we can be completely honest about ourselves. God knows that; Jesus knows that, so He left us a visible Church and, in that Church, a Sacrament of Reconciliation with the practice of confession.

Some people might say, "Well, I've gone to confession many times, but I don't see any real change in my life." The question is, "Do you really want a change?" It doesn't happen automatically. Repentance includes *desire for conversion* and for repairing wrongs—calling on God's grace to bring it about. It's not a question of a promise—but a firm resolution to accomplish it. If there is no sorrow and no intention to behave differently, nothing happens. It's just going through the motions.

There are times when we don't really get in touch with what needs to be confessed. A priest will often run across the attitude: "Sure I've been away for twenty years, but I don't have any sins. All I did was cuss a few times." Wow! Twenty years, and all you did was cuss! I've got more than that to confess in one week. Pius XII was Pope when I was ordained in 1950. If back then he said,

"The greatest sin of our day is the denial of sin itself," how much truer is it now? Nobody sins anymore! No wonder there's no rush on the confessional.

If you can't think of any sins, for a starter take another look at the Ten Commandments, the Beatitudes (Mt 5:3-11, Lk 6:20-26), or pick up some written form of an examination of conscience. Think about your life right now—the circumstances, challenges, and responsibilities. What are you doing? What are you not doing about it all? Bring that for confession.

On the other hand, if you do your best and you can't think of anything, just go in humbly and say, "Father, I'm blank. I can't think of anything right now, but I know I'm a sinner. I know it's only through Jesus that I can get to heaven. I'm asking for His mercy and forgiveness, and I'm sorry for all the sins of my life." That would be sufficient. In fact, it's good to say in every confession, after telling your sins, "I'm sorry for these and all the sins of my whole life."

In the past, we used to hear more often about the seven capital or root sins. They are pride, covetousness, lust, anger, gluttony, envy, and laziness. The first time I heard somebody talk about them, I said to myself, "Wow! I've got 'em all!" I think we all struggle with all of them, but there's usually one that is our underlying and predominant fault. After we confess the sins that come to mind, especially anything that is a serious or mortal sin, it would be good to say very humbly, "And this is the most important thing in my life that needs to change." It might be one of the above or something else, but **try to get in touch with the main thing that's holding you back or that keeps tripping you up—the main thing that you're doing that is not according to God's will, or the main thing that He's calling you to do that you're neglecting.** Name "the demon." Express it the best you can.

OVERCOMING FEAR

There are still people who have a fear of confession because of embarrassment. They wonder, "What will the priest think of me?" Well, since I'm a priest for over half a century, let me tell you what

I'd think of you. (And I know enough about my brother priests to know that this is what the average priest would also tell you.) Suppose someone has been away from confession for a very long time, someone carrying a heavy load of sin—things they're ashamed of and have never been able to tell. Then, they finally get it out. They say it, and lay that burden down. Do you know the way I feel? *That's one of the happiest moments in my life as a priest.* That's why I became a priest. It's like a doctor. You don't go through all that education and training just to put band-aids on people. When someone comes along who's really hurting and you're able to help that person in a significant way, you feel it's worth it all! So, never deliberately hold back anything serious in confession. If you forget, that's different. The absolution covers that (but mention it in your next confession if it's serious). Don't even try to "pretty up" your sins. Just tell it like it is—the simpler the better.

In my parish and as I go about giving missions, retreats, etc., one of the best things that happens occurs in the reconciliation room. The chains that are broken, the windows that are opened, the new life that breaks through! God has a special grace and blessing waiting for you in this sacrament. You'll miss it unless you come. Just come, opening the doors of your heart and lips in honesty and humility to receive it—not only once, but regularly.

In my own parish, the pastor, a former Lutheran minister, has strongly encouraged frequent confession. He makes himself available before all his Masses, with an amazing response from his people. Throughout my life as a priest, I've personally made use of the Sacrament of Reconciliation (with spiritual direction) every month. I've experienced its on-going, life-saving, and balancing power over and over. It's been like that *"balm in Gilead"* (Jer 8:22) "that saves the sin-sick soul (and) makes the wounded whole." Though we are only obliged to go to confession when there is serious sin, I'd recommend monthly confession (if not more often) to everyone. Ever since his first encyclical letter, Pope John Paul II has stressed frequent confession. I understand he goes weekly and that Mother Teresa of Calcutta did the same.

AN EXAMINATION OF CONSCIENCE
BEFORE CONFESSION

Lord Jesus, I come before You. I come before Your cross. I am a sinner. Your name is Jesus. Your name means Savior. Jesus, I open my heart and life to You. I ask Your forgiveness. I ask Your transforming and amazing grace. I ask You to take over and be the Lord of my life.

Lord, there are many ways I could examine my conscience. I'll just use a simple one right now—the commandment you said was the greatest and includes all the others: *"Love the Lord, your God, with all your heart, with all your soul, and with all your mind...love your neighbor as yourself"* (Mt 22:37-40). Do I love You with all my heart? Lord, I know I don't. I don't know how many of us can say, *"with all my heart...all my mind."* You know my half-heartedness and holding back. You're asking, "Do you want a new heart? Is that the direction your life is moving in? Do you understand that if I give you even one more day, it's so that you can grow in love, realizing more and more every day My love for you?"

Are you, Jesus, truly Lord of my life? Do I hand over everything to you, or are there areas of my life that I never even talk about with you? How much time and attention do I give to prayer, to the Scriptures and other spiritual reading, and to learning more and more about my Catholic faith? St. Jerome said, "Ignorance of the Scriptures is ignorance of Christ." Can I afford to be ignorant of you? St. Peter urged us to *"Always be ready to give an explanation to anyone who asks you for a reason for your hope"* (1Pt 3:15). Am I preparing myself more and more to do that?

What about the love of neighbor, Lord? Is there someone about whom I say, "Well, I forgave 'em—but I won't forget it!" What kind of forgiveness is that? I *can have a new heart,* and I can pray that others will also—if I open my heart to you.

What about my family, neighbors, fellow workers, or parishioners, Lord? Do I complain that they don't show me much love? What is that going to sound like on the day of judgment? You're not going to ask me what **they** did. You're going to ask me

The Gift Of His Church

what I did with the short time you gave me. As St. John of the Cross said, "Where there is no love, put love, and you will find love." My mission is to go on loving, and I'm never a sucker for doing that! You said that whatever you do for anyone, you do it for Me (Mt 25:40). You'll receive it, Lord, and that's all that matters.

What about my congregation and parish? Do I get involved, or do I just sit back and let others do the job? Do I only criticize and cause ill feelings and division? Do I encourage, affirm, and try to bring people together? When necessary, do I deal with abuses constructively and in a Christian manner?

What about the community at large? Do I even take the trouble to vote conscientiously? Do I ever write a letter or make a phone call—complimenting something good or hoping to correct something harmful?

What about the world in which I live? If destruction or starvation threatens many—it's my world, Lord. I can't do everything, but I can do something. I can offer my prayer, sacrifice, and growth in love. I can share my few loaves and fishes and let you multiply them (e.g. Jn 6:1-15).

What about that love of self? That's a part of your command that we of *your neighbor as yourself*." Do I accept myself as you made me, or do I go through life wanting to be someone I was never intended to be? Do I even do the things that a doctor says are necessary for my health? Am I gentle with myself? Do I take time for good, wholesome, and healthy relationships and friendships? Am I using my mind productively or just letting it rot in front of the TV set? Am I growing as a person—growing especially in love of you, my God, and of my neighbor? What is the main thing that I am doing or not doing that's tripping me up in that regard? Lord, help me to be truly sorry for my sins and firmly resolved not to continue sinning—relying on your saving grace.

I know that I don't have to cry in order to be truly sorry, but as I kneel here in spirit beneath your cross and look up to you, I realize that if there is anything in life that I should ever cry about, it is because I have offended you, my God, who are so good and deserving of all my love! So I open my heart to you and pray.

Love's the Message that I Heard

O my God, I am heartily sorry for having offended you, and I detest all my sins because of your just punishments, but most of all because they have offended you, my God, who art all good and deserving of all my love. I firmly resolve, with the help of your grace, to sin no more and to avoid the near occasions of sin. AMEN

CHAPTER 5
Mission Impossible Made Possible

The Holy Spirit

"*The Holy Spirit will come upon you, and the power of the Most High will overshadow you...for nothing will be impossible for God...*(and) *Mary said...May it be done to me according to your word*" (Lk. 1:35 & 38).

"Come, Holy Spirit, fill the hearts of your faithful and enkindle in us the fire of your love."

WHY DO WE NEED THE HOLY SPIRIT?

Years ago, I had a chance to visit the site in Jerusalem that commemorates the first Pentecost when the room was shaken and the tongues of fire appeared. From that room, the apostles went out to begin the mission Jesus had entrusted to them, fired up, enlightened and strengthened by the Holy Spirit (Acts 2). Down through the centuries, that mission of the Lord has continued in His Church through the power of the Spirit. At the beginning of the Second Vatican Council, Pope John XXIII prayed that, in this our day, we could experience a new Pentecost. Pope John Paul II earnestly echoes that prayer. We need the same Holy Spirit today as much as ever. In fact, all the things we've talked about in the previous chapters can become a growing reality in our daily lives only through the power of the Spirit. How about a rapid review?

In the first chapter, we spoke about **God as our Father** and His amazing love and care for each of us. That's great stuff, but how do we let it all sink into our hard hearts and thick skulls? How do we stay conscious of it in our hectic noisy lives? The secret is the Holy Spirit, who dwells in our hearts. St. Paul says, "*All who are led by the Spirit of God are sons of God. You did not receive a spirit of slavery leading you back into fear, but a spirit of adoption*

121

through which we cry out, 'Abba' (that is, 'Father'). The Spirit himself gives witness with our spirit that we are children of God" (Rom 8:14-16 NAB/unrevised). The Holy Spirit can bring us to an ever growing consciousness of who we are as God's children and what it means when we cry, "Abba, Father."

Next, we talked about **Jesus Christ as our Brother, our Savior, our Lord, and our God.** We especially emphasized how important it is to let Jesus be the Lord of our lives. Whether we recognize Him or not, He is the Lord, and, because He is, we're called to personally and freely surrender ourselves and everything in our lives to Him. That's not easy, because we want to be our own lords. **We** want to be in control instead of saying, "Lord, you take over." To say that and mean it does not annihilate free will but opens the door to the highest freedom to do what God wants instead of just what we want, to be all He wants us to be, and to be used by Him to accomplish His work in this world.

Being the self-centered and self-willed sinners that we are, how can we do that? Again, the secret is through the Holy Spirit. In 1st Corinthians 12:3, Paul says, *"No one can say, 'Jesus is Lord,' except by the holy Spirit."* No one can say it, believe it, and live it except by the Holy Spirit.

In the third chapter, we talked about **prayer, personal and communal.** We need the Holy Spirit to help us become people of prayer, to persevere in prayer when it is difficult and dry, and to pray from our hearts, not just from our lips. Paul says that in the 8th chapter of his letter to the Romans, *"The Spirit too helps us in our weakness, for we do not know how to pray as we ought; but the Spirit himself makes intercession for us with groanings that cannot be expressed in speech. He who searches hearts knows what the Spirit means, for the Spirit intercedes for the saints as God himself wills"* (vv 26-27 NAB unrevised).

What is meant by that passage, *"groanings that cannot be expressed in speech"*? It could well be related to the experience of praying or speaking in tongues.

When some people hear about that, they say, "Man, that sounds way out to me." Years ago, I would have said the same thing, but it's right there in the Scriptures. (Since it's so misunderstood, I'll say something about it.) In the 14th chapter of Paul's first letter to the Corinthians—I once counted it—tongues are mentioned sixteen times! Paul says, "*I should like all of you to speak in tongues*" and "*I speak in tongues more than any of you*" (1 Cor 14:5 & 18). Well, if it was good enough for St. Paul, then why knock it? Maybe you don't understand it, but keep an open mind and heart.

St. Paul makes a distinction between praying in tongues and speaking in tongues, affirming and giving guidance about both. *Speaking in tongues* is delivering a message (often a word of encouragement) from the Lord, which Paul says is useless unless the speaker or someone else present can interpret it. *Praying in tongues* (much more common than the above) is different. Deep within our hearts, there are things that you and I want to express to God—profound yearnings, thanksgivings, and needs in our lives. They're too deep or too big to put into words, so sometimes we just bypass the words and let the sounds or "groanings" come forth.

Words are artificial. You and I had to learn from someone else to call an object "book" or "table" or "pencil." Very small children don't use words. Sounds just bubble up from their hearts before they learn to speak, and those sounds convey their thoughts and feelings. That is the way I understand the experience of praying in tongues. It is not something that is entirely beyond our control. (You don't just start babbling as you're standing in the check-out line at the supermarket!) You can start or stop at will. You can choose to open your mouth, move your tongue, and let the sounds emerge, but the sounds are not just of your own creation. They are an expression of the Holy Spirit praying within you.

In any case, Paul tells us that, *to be people of prayer, we need the help of the Holy Spirit.* I experience that help over and over when I pray with and for others, asking the Holy Spirit to guide me. Things come to mind that I know I would never have thought of on my own.

The fourth area covered was **the Church, emphasizing reconciliation and unity**—unity of faith, love, witnessing, and working together. Only the Holy Spirit can bring that about. Paul says that in the fourth chapter of his letter to the Ephesians, "*Make every effort to preserve the unity which has the Spirit as its origin* *and peace as its binding force"* (v 3, NAB unrevised). This last chapter will concentrate entirely on the Holy Spirit—"the Soul of the Church."

Paul talks about the works of the Spirit and what the Holy Spirit brings about in the life of the Church. *"There are different kinds of spiritual gifts, but the same Spirit; there are different forms of service, but the same Lord; there are different workings, but the same God, who produces all of them in everyone. To each individual, the manifestation of the Spirit is given for some benefit. To one is given, through the Spirit, the expression of wisdom; to another, the expression of knowledge, according to the same Spirit; to another, faith by the same Spirit; to another, gifts of healing by the one Spirit; to another, mighty deeds; to another, prophecy; to another discernment of spirits; to another, varieties of tongues; to another interpretation of tongues. But one and the same Spirit produces all of these, distributing them individually to each person as he wishes"* (1Cor 12:4-11).

Each one of us is offered different gifts of the Spirit. The above list is only partial; many more could be added. Open to the Spirit, we each have special gifts to contribute to the work of God's Church. Someone put it this way, "None of us has it all together, but, together, we have it all." (I worry about people who think they have it all together!) I have a gift; you have a gift; your neighbor has a gift. One has something the other doesn't have. When we put them together, we have enough gifts to accomplish in this world the mission of His Body, the Church.

In Paul's letter to the Galatians, he lists fruits or characteristics produced by the Spirit. *"The fruit of the Spirit is love, joy, peace, patience, kindness, generosity, faithfulness, gentleness, and self-control"* (1:22). Wow! The Holy Spirit can really do something!

So we pray, "Come Holy Spirit, fill the hearts of your faithful. Enkindle in us the fire of your love, and we will be re-created, and you will renew the face of the earth!" At the dawn of a new millennium, we cry out for the whole Church of God to come alive in the Spirit, opening and surrendering our lives to Him more and more every day.

THE HOLY SPIRIT IN THE OLD AND NEW TESTAMENTS

The mystery of the Holy Trinity, the mystery of God's inner life, was not revealed until the coming of Jesus to this earth. The eternal Son of God took flesh and walked among us. In many ways and different words, He made known the mystery of Father, Son, and Holy Spirit—one God and three persons possessing the one divine nature. He revealed His own divine Sonship and the Holy Spirit as one God with Father and Son (e.g. Mt 28:19). Though this revelation was unique to Jesus, there are at least foreshadowings of it in the Old Testament.

In the thirty-sixth chapter of the Book of Ezekiel, the Jews are in exile. God makes a promise to His people through the prophet Ezekiel. *"I will take you away from among the nations, gather you from all the foreign lands, bring you back to your own land. I will sprinkle clean water upon you, to cleanse you from all your impurities. From all your idols I will cleanse you. I will give you a new heart and place a new spirit within you, taking from your bodies your stony hearts and giving you natural hearts. I will put my spirit within you and make you live by my statutes. You shall live in the land I gave your fathers. You shall be my people, and I will be your God"* (vv 24-28).

The Israelites did come back from exile, but, like so many passages in the Old Testament, the words and the event were a type of what was to be realized fully in Jesus and His gift of the Spirit. The new heart and the outpouring of the Spirit that He promised were experienced especially at Pentecost, but they are meant to be experienced throughout the life of the Church as we open our hearts to the same Spirit.

Jesus talked so many times about the Holy Spirit, especially towards the end of His earthly life. Over and over again, He tells us that He is going away, but that He will send the Holy Spirit. We find these words particularly in the Last Supper discourse of Jesus beginning with the fourteenth chapter of John's Gospel. He says, *"I will ask the Father, and He will give you another Paraclete to be with you always: the Spirit of truth, whom the world cannot ac-*

cept, since it neither sees him nor recognizes him; but you can recognize him because he remains with you and will be within you. I will not leave you orphaned; I will come back to you" (v 16-18 NAB unrevised). In that same chapter, He continues, "The Advocate, the holy Spirit that the Father will send in my name—he will teach you everything and remind you of all that (I) told you" (v. 26). At the end of the fifteenth chapter, Jesus says, "When the Advocate comes whom I will send you from the Father, the Spirit of truth that proceeds from the Father, he will testify to me. And you also testify..." (v 26).

Have you ever thought to yourself, "Wouldn't it be wonderful if Jesus had stayed on the earth? If He were here right now, He'd straighten out the mess we're in. He'd bring us back to our senses and show us the way." Well, listen to what Jesus says about that. We find it in the sixteenth chapter of John's Gospel. *"But I tell you the truth,* **it is better for you that I go.** *For if I do not go, the Advocate will not come to you. But if I go, I will send him to you"* (v.7).

You see, the plan of God is not for Jesus to stay around, but for you and me to stay around. In every age and day, the people of God, filled with His Spirit, are commissioned to continue the work of Jesus. We are the body of Christ on earth.

Jesus says of us, His Church, *"Amen, Amen, I say to you, whoever believes in me will do the works that I do and will do greater ones than these..."* (Jn 14:12). What an amazing statement. Through the power of the Spirit, the Spirit of Jesus, we, as the Church of God, are meant to continue His mission and even, in a sense, do greater things on this earth than He did.

Near the beginning of the Acts of the Apostles, we find one of the last promises Jesus made to us. *"While meeting with them, He enjoined them not to depart from Jerusalem, but to wait for 'the promise of the Father about which you have heard me speak; for John baptized with water, but in a few days, you will be baptized with the holy Spirit...you will receive power when the holy Spirit comes upon you, and you will be my witnesses in Jerusalem, throughout Judea, and Samaria...'* (And in New York, Chicago, New Orleans, and Turkey Creek—you didn't know that was in there, did you?) *'...and even to the ends of the earth'"* (vv 4,5,8).

YOU WILL BE WITNESSES

For years I read the Scriptures, and I thought of them as an account of what happened a long time ago. Then, somewhere along the line, it began to dawn on me. Scripture is inspired by God, handed down to us, and read by us, because it's **meant** for us—**today**. We need to see ourselves in it, and hear in it the message that God is speaking to us right now. He's saying, *"You* (who are reading this now) *will be my witnesses."* He's counting on **you** as He counted on those first witnesses, those first disciples and apostles.

In that famous apostolic exhortation, *Evangelization in the Modern World,* Pope Paul VI said that what the world needs is not so much teachers as witnesses—and teachers who are also witnesses. What does it mean to be a witness? Here's just another example.

During my first pastorate, I had a visit one day from a beautiful young girl of around seventeen or eighteen whose family belonged to our parish. Her story went something like this. "Father, I stopped going to church. My mother would go, and she was constantly bugging me, 'Go to church; go to church.' But when I looked at my mother, she was always so sad and 'down in the mouth'. She seemed to be worried all the time, especially about how to pay the bills. I thought to myself, 'Why go to church? What good is it doing my mother? She still comes home troubled and glum.' Then, I saw something remarkable happen. My mother started going to those weekly prayer meetings at the parish house. When she came home, she was singing around our house all the day long. No longer worried, she would say things like, 'God's our Father. He's got the whole world in His hands. He watches over the tiniest sparrow; He'll certainly take care of us. All I have to do is what I can, trusting Him and putting it all in His hands.'

"I thought to myself, 'Wow! If God and the Church can do that for my mother, there must be something to this.' So, I've started back to church. In fact, I'm so excited about what God and His Church can do, I'm here today to ask if I can be one of the religion teachers!"

You see, that mother no longer had to preach. She became a witness. The girl saw God alive in her mother. She saw the effects of the Spirit in her mother's life, and she wanted it in her own. That's the way Christianity spread in the beginning. People looked at those first Christians and said, "There's something different about them—a new honesty, integrity, humility, and a love we haven't known. There's a joy and a trust in God, and we want that." Even in our fumbling and our fears, like that mother, you and I are called to be witnesses for Him. To be witnesses, we need the power of the Holy Spirit.

COMIC RELIEF AND DIRECTION

So our prayer is "Come Holy Spirit." What are we asking for and expecting when we pray that prayer? Along those lines, the story is told about the preacher who planned to give a dramatic sermon on the Holy Spirit and stationed a boy in the choir loft with a dove (a biblical symbol of the Holy Spirit) enclosed in a little cage. He told the boy that he was going to preach about the Holy Spirit and that, at the climax of his sermon when everyone was excited, he would cry, "Come Holy Spirit!" That would be the signal for the boy to open the cage and let the dove fly over the congregation. Everyone would exclaim, "See! The Spirit has come to us in the form of a dove!"

That night, the minister got into his sermon, and when everyone was duly worked up, he proceeded to cry, "Come Holy Spirit!" But nothing happened. Thinking the boy didn't hear him, he cried louder. When still there was nothing, he figured the boy must have gone to sleep, so he cried again at the top of his voice. At that, the boy stuck his head out of the choir loft and yelled back, "The cat got the bird!"

We're not expecting the Holy Spirit to come flying from out of the blue in some visible form. Where then are we going with all this talk about the Spirit? The goal is twofold: (1) a growing awareness of His presence in our hearts and lives, and (2) an ever-increasing surrender to the Spirit.

AWARENESS OF THE SPIRIT

If you're in God's grace, trying to live for God and do His will, you are a living *"temple of the holy Spirit"* (1 Cor 6:19). My mother shared this with me in those latter years of her long life. "Bobby, when I was a younger woman, I didn't think that much about the Holy Spirit, but now that I've gotten older, I think a lot about the Holy Spirit." A priest who was in his seventies also told me something like that on one retreat, and, on another, a nun who had just celebrated her fiftieth jubilee. I think that's what happens when we walk with God; we become more aware of those deep realities of our faith and their meaning in our lives.

The fourth chapter of John's Gospel tells of Jesus' meeting with a woman at the well in Samaria. He said, referring to the Holy Spirit, *"If you knew the gift of God and who is saying to you, 'Give me a drink,' you would have asked him and he would have given you living water… the water I shall give will become in him a spring of water welling up to eternal life"* (vv 10 & 14).

I saw that in my mother. St. Paul says, *"Even though my body wastes away, my inner spirit grows stronger, day after day"* (2 Cor 4:16). In my mother's old age, as her physical frame withered away, her inner spirit was shining through all the more. The night she died, she was talking in French about "La vie eternelle." Somebody asked, "What is that?" and she answered, "That's eternal life." When the person asked again, "Did you say 'eternal light'?" this ninety-six-year-old woman, frail as she could be and about to breathe her last, says, as clear as a bell, "Not light, life: L-I-F-E," spelling it out letter by letter. She added that she was going. When there was an attempt to reassure her that she wasn't going anywhere, she answered with certainty, "Oh, yes I am! You want to come?" She was *excited* about eternal life and experiencing that *"spring of water"* that bubbles up to life everlasting!

Use your imagination for a bit. Suppose Jesus was still on earth traveling about. You get a phone call at home, and He asks if you could give Him lodging for the night. What would you say? Well, after you got over the shock, you'd probably say, "By all means, Lord, come on over." Then what would you do? (Why is it that, whenever I ask that on parish missions, I always get the response, "I'd straighten up the house"?)

So, Jesus arrives. He knocks at the door and waits for you to answer. (He never pushes His way in.) So, you open the door and say, "Come on in, Lord. A hearty welcome!" Then you show Him to His room. "You can use this room, Lord. I've asked my son to sleep on the sofa tonight. I hope it's all right." "Oh sure," He says. Then, would you close the door and just forget about Him? No way!

Before He ever got there, you'd probably get on the telephone and call up relatives, friends, and neighbors. "Come on over," you'd say. "Jesus Christ is going to be a guest in our house tonight!" Then, you'd gather around the kitchen table or in the den and sit at the Master's feet. All night long, you'd ask Him those questions you always wanted to ask, and you'd bring Him all those needs that you know He alone can handle.

Why do I tell you that? Listen to what Jesus says in the fourteenth chapter of St. John. *"If anyone loves me, my Father will love him, and we will come to him and take up our dwelling with him"* (v 28). If you love God and are trying to do His will, if you've repented of your sins and are in the state of grace, you are *"the temple of God" (*1 Cor 3:16*).* The living God—Father, Son, and Holy Spirit (since you can't separate the Trinity)—dwells within the house of your heart right now.

He's there as long as you make room for Him—but He won't be an unwelcomed guest. If you choose something that's incompatible with His presence (and that's what mortal sin is), the two can't be present in the same place at the same time. Realizing this, we can turn back to Him and say, "Lord, I made a fool out of myself. I chose a creature in place of the Creator. I'm sorry for offending you, who are so good and *deserving of all my love.* I let that go and open my heart once again to you." Then He comes anew, never to leave as long as you welcome Him.

Don't close Him up though in some little corner of your life or your heart and forget all about Him. He's there for you. He's there every day to enlighten and guide you. He's there to give you the strength and courage, purity, love, and joy that you need. Call upon Him. Communicate with Him. Rejoice in His presence. Become more and more aware of your special invited guest. That's the first thing to remember: you're "*a temple of the holy Spirit.*" The second is to surrender yourself wholeheartedly to the promptings and the workings of the Spirit within you.

SURRENDERING TO THE SPIRIT

During my first pastorate, I tried my hand at sailing. I was using a small single-sail boat designed primarily for just one person. I turned over a number of times in the choppy waters of Lake Pontchartrain but did better on calmer Bayou Des Allemands. I never became much of a sailor, but I did get this brilliant insight: *you've got to open the sail!*

Let the wind catch it and move you along. That's also true of the Holy Spirit. Many of us are continually working our heads off, pulling at the oars of life, and trying to do it all by ourselves. God certainly wants our cooperation and best effort, but the main thing He asks is that we entrust ourselves to Him and open our hearts to the wind and fire of His Spirit. "Let go and let God." So many people down through the ages have testimonies of what happened in their lives when they did just that. Let me just share my own with you.

When I was working as an assistant under several different pastors, in my young pride, I would sometimes think, "Hey, I could do it better than this guy!" (Now, I identify with the new young pastor who told me, "It's funny, but the day after I became a pastor, my whole attitude towards pastors changed!") I looked forward to the day when I would be a pastor and could implement all those wonderful dreams and plans I had for a parish of my own.

Finally, in the early sixties, that day came. The Archbishop called me in and appointed me to my first pastorate—about thirty miles west of New Orleans along the mighty Mississippi (in early days called "the river of the Holy Spirit"). I was a happy man! Now, all those dreams and plans could be realized.

As the months and then the years went by, I saw that a lot of the dreams were not being worked out. There were racial divisions in the parish and community at large, and I wanted so much to bring people together—black and white. From the time I was a young child, my parents and Church had instilled in me the conviction that we were all God's children and had to put that into practice by truly acting like brothers and sisters to one another. I was also convinced that, if we couldn't get together in the family of the Church, how could we ever have that hope for the whole human family? It looked like the more I said or did about all this in the parish or civic community, the more tensions increased and divisions solidified. There were also problems in our parish staff (not for racial reasons but maybe just my own ineptitude). There, too, I couldn't get it together to accomplish fully the work I thought we were called to do.

To add to this, I came down with a bad case of the flu. Even after I got over it, I felt physically drained. I couldn't get my strength back. I had lost my drive, my "zip." I began to question myself, my ability, and my manhood. I felt like a failure, a "washout"—like I just couldn't do the job or "cut the mustard."

Around that time, I went off on vacation and took with me a couple of things to read about the Holy Spirit. Of course, I had always believed in the Holy Spirit and regularly invoked His help through the years. In fact, in connection with my ordination and first Mass, I had distributed little prayer cards with Cardinal Mercier's anointed prayer to the Holy Spirit. I had prayed this prayer, especially in times of decision, throughout my life as a priest and continue to share it with others.

> Holy Spirit, soul of my soul, I adore thee. Enlighten, guide, strengthen, and console me. Tell me what I ought to do and command me to do it. I ask for nothing except to be submissive to whatever you permit to happen to me. Only show me what is your will. (With adaptation.)

So, even though I had been aware of and devoted to the Holy Spirit for many years, there was something new in what I was reading on that vacation. *I was encountering real life stories of people of our day* and the new and exciting things happening to them when

Mission Impossible Made Possible

they committed their lives to Jesus as Lord and surrendered themselves to the Holy Spirit.

This was brought home to me particularly by a little paperback book called *The Cross and the Switchblade*. It's the story of a young clergyman who was inspired to go into New York city and reach out to members of teenage gangs hung up on dope, sex, or violence. In spite of his fear, hesitation, and initial failure, he continued to rely on God rather than on himself. Eventually, one gang leader responded to his efforts, opened his life to Jesus Christ and His Spirit, and was able to kick an addiction to hard drugs. Others followed, and a whole new outreach movement to such teenagers began.

In those days, I wasn't accustomed to letting my emotions show. I had grown up believing men don't cry; it wasn't "macho." As I read that book, however, tears welled up in my eyes. I was identifying with the minister in the story. For the first time in my life, *I was acutely experiencing and admitting my own limitations in the face of a task bigger than myself.* I was coming to learn firsthand what it means to rely on the power of God.

After I got back from vacation, but before I returned to the parish, I went to see a priest friend in our area who had started a small Catholic Charismatic prayer group, and he brought me over to meet the prayer group leader. As we sat in the parlor of this lady's home, they shared with me what God was doing in the lives of members of that group as they came together, week after week, to pray and praise and open their lives to the Holy Spirit. Before I left that house, I did something that I had not planned on doing.

In effect, I told them, "In a few days, I'm going back to my parish. I know that the same problems will be there as when I left, but I know something now that I didn't know before. *I know how much I need the Holy Spirit.* When I was baptized, confirmed, and ordained, I believe that I did receive special outpourings of God's Holy Spirit, but in those days I didn't know how much I needed the Spirit. In the back of my mind, I must have thought that I could do it—with a little help from God. Now, I've been knocked down enough to know I can't do it, but I believe that God can do it. *If I could only let go and let God take over,* getting out of the way and

133

letting Him act in me and through me, then it will happen."

I asked them to pray for the removal of any barriers in me that interfered with the workings of His Spirit. I remember one of them saying, "You're asking to die!" (i.e. to yourself so that God can take over). So, I knelt down, and they gathered around me—my priest friend, this mother of a family, and a young student who was a member of the prayer group (now a priest) and happened to show up right at that time. They placed their hands on me and prayed. Do you know what happened? Nothing happened! (I thought.) I went away from that house as dry as dry bones!

As I walked out to my car, I do remember experiencing something to which I gave little attention—a burning sensation, like a little pilot light ignited in the middle of my chest (or the depth of my heart). When I awoke the next morning, I was singing. Now, that's a miracle! I'm not a morning person. I can stay up late at night but hate to get up early in the morning. In those days, especially, I didn't feel like singing when I got up, but that morning I was singing. In fact, I began singing in my dream even before I opened my eyes. It was verses of a song about the Holy Spirit by Miriam Therese recorded by the Medical Mission Sisters:

> Spirit of God in the clear running water,
> Blowing to greatness the trees on the hill.
> Spirit of God in the finger of morning:
> Fill the earth, bring it to birth,
> And blow where You will.
> Blow, blow, blow 'til I be
> But breath of the Spirit blowing in me.
>
> Spirit of God every man's heart is lonely,
> Watching and waiting and hungry until,
> Spirit of God, we long that You only.
> Fulfill the earth, bring it to birth,
> And blow where You will.
> Blow, blow, blow 'til I be,
> But breath of the Spirit blowing in me.

Mission Impossible Made Possible

A few days later when I got back to my parish, I noticed there was something different in my life. There was a new joy and enthusiasm in my work as a priest. There was a new realization that God was not a million miles away; He was right with me and within me. There was a new love for the people God had called me to serve and a new acceptance of myself—with all my shortcomings as well as my gifts. There was a new thanksgiving that was welling up within me, thanking God for everything—eventually even for the difficult and painful things, believing His hand was also at work in them.

When I picked up the Scriptures, things that I had read many times before seemed to take on greater depths of meaning. As I began again my work as pastor, it seemed as if God were at work in a new way. There was a new power in ministry, and I knew it wasn't any power of my own. It was simply that I was not relying as much on myself. I was relying on Him to do what needed to be done—getting out of the way and not blocking Him as much—and He was coming through in a new and wonderful way.

Since then, there has grown in me a burning desire to share with all my brothers and sisters—with everyone in the world—the Good News about God our Father, His Son Jesus Christ and His Church, the new way of life to which we're called, and the power of the Holy Spirit to help us live it. The Holy Spirit has given me a new appreciation of everything in my Catholic faith. I believe the mission and evangelization work and what I'm sharing with you right now were all prompted by Him.

The Holy Spirit doesn't just want to do some little thing in your life and mine—to *"patch up an old garment"* (Mk 2:21-22). No, He wants to do an amazing new thing in and through us. He wants to give each of us a whole new garment—a new life and a new heart (Ez 36:24-28).

Ever since I was a child, I had prayed with fellow Catholics that old familiar prayer: "Come Holy Spirit, fill the hearts of your faithful. Enkindle in us the fire of Your love, and we will be recreated and **you** will renew the face of the earth." I still say that prayer today. What's new now is that, when I repeat those words, **I really expect the Holy Spirit to stir up that fire.** He wants to

135

Love's the Message that I Heard

set our hearts on fire and use us as bold witnesses for Him. He wants to renew us, His Church, His world, and use us in His mission of renewing "the face of the earth!"

What is our part in all this? It is to open ourselves and surrender ourselves continually to Him. It is to persevere in praying from our hearts: "Come Holy Spirit!" It is to *expect* that He will indeed answer that prayer as we let go of the barriers more and more and surrender to Him. Then, the things that seem to be impossible become possible, because *"nothing will be impossible for God"* (Lk 1:37).

There's so much that needs to be done—enormous tasks, challenging work. We wonder how we can ever accomplish it. We dream beautiful dreams at times and hear inspiring testimonies. We ask, "How could I ever do that? It seems so good, but how can I put it into practice in my marriage, my single life, my family, my business, my Church, or my world? How can I be a witness? I'm so timid and afraid. I'm still smarting under past hurts and wonder if I'll ever be healed." The answer is that **you can't do it, but God can**—and He can use you if you just let Him. Nothing is impossible with God. *"If you knew the gift of God...you would have asked him...."* (Jn 4:10).

The power of God is available to you and me. We're a bunch of dummies and incompetents when we just rely on ourselves. We'll never get the job done. When we rely on God, the weaker we are, the more effectively we can witness to the power of God; *"...for when I am weak, then I am strong"* Paul says. *"I will rather boast most gladly of **my weaknesses, in order that the power of Christ may dwell with me**"* (2 Cor 12:9-10).

Just look at the history of the Church, beginning back in the Old Testament. What did Moses say to God? *"Who am I that I should go to Pharaoh and lead the Israelites out of Egypt?"* God's answer is, *"I will be with you..."* (Ex 3:11-12). "They'll know it's my power and not yours."

So many of the canonized saints testify to the same. When they were called to do something, they thought of others who were more capable, but God said, "I want you." That young virgin of Nazareth, when called upon for the most important role of all, asked how it was possible. Gabriel answered, *"The Holy Spirit will come upon you, and the power of the Most High will overshadow you...for nothing will be impossible for God."* Mary responded, *"Behold, I am the handmaid of the Lord. May it be done to me according to your word"* (Luke 1:35-38).

The same Holy Spirit will also come upon you. The power of the Most High will overshadow you. Nothing is impossible with God. If you hesitate, just look to Mary for inspiration and prayerful help. Then say, "I am your servant, Lord. Just use me."

PRAYER

"O, Lord Jesus Christ, once again I come to You, the one and only Savior and Lord of this world. I open my heart to You right now. I acknowledge You as Savior, as Lord, and as God in the flesh. Forgive me all my sins and timidity. I'm sorry for offending you, who are so good and deserving of all my love. Remove the barriers that keep me from You. Break the chains that bind me. Take me from myself and give me to Thyself.

You promised me the gift of your Spirit. You promised to renew my life and to renew the face of the earth. Revive me and renew me so that You can use me.

Expectantly, I pray 'Come Holy Spirit. Fill the hearts of your faithful. Enkindle in me and in us the fire of your love, and we shall be re-created, and you will renew the face of the earth.' Amen. Alleluia!"

Love's the Message that I Heard

APPENDIX

PRAYER FOR THE INNER HEALING OF MEMORIES

(The following prayer is only an example. You could use your own. In praying it, if you have a good imagination, use it. If not, God's power to heal is still present. If anything in the prayer triggers images, thoughts, or emotions too disturbing to handle—just pass over that part, commending it to the Lord. You could come back to it at another time. Healing is a lifetime process. Pray for it often.)

Loving Father, *"You formed my inmost being; you knit me in my mother's womb. I praise you, so wonderfully you made me"* (Ps 139:13-14). Psychiatrists tell us that the infant child even in the mother's womb begins to pick up sensations of being wanted or unwanted, loved or unloved, of anxiety or peace according to the disposition of the mother and others associated with her. But Lord, no matter what those conditions may have been—especially if I've wondered whether or not I was truly wanted—you tell me: "Forget it! I wanted you. I formed you. *'I have called you by name; you are mine...Because you are precious in my eyes and glorious and because I love you'"* (Is 43:1 & 4). Lord, all is possible for you and all is present to you as if it were happening at this moment. Whatever may have gone wrong in the depth of the womb or whatever was missing that I needed at that very early time, I believe that you, for whom all is possible, can heal it right now, and you can fill up within me all that was absent—all the love, warmth, and security that was needed. I ask you to begin to do that at this moment as I picture your loving hand forming and caressing me. *(Pause.)*

As I picture myself being born into the world, wherever it may have been, crying, hungry, helpless, I picture you, Jesus, as the unseen Doctor in that place, taking me into your arms and pressing me to your Sacred Heart, welcoming me joyfully into the world, and warming me with your love. *(Pause.)* I also picture you, Jesus, handing me with great care to Mary, your mother and mine. She lovingly takes me into her arms and presses me to her Immaculate Heart, filling up inside of me anything missing of a mother's love. *(Pause).*

I see myself now as a little child needing the embrace and affirmation of father, mother, big brother, or sister. I picture you, Jesus, lifting me onto your lap or bouncing me on your knee, stroking or mussing up my hair, listening to my chatter, pressing me to your heart as you must have done with the children in the Gospel. You tell me of your love and the Father's love, of your delight in me and the wonderful plans you have for me in this life and the next... *(Pause.)* Then, Jesus, you again hand me over to my mother, Mary, who picks me up and does with me much the same—but in the way only a mother would do. Your love and Mary's love, acceptance, and affirmation are sufficient to fill up inside of me all that may have been missing in those years of my life. *(Pause.)*

As the years roll on, I see myself as a teenager in that often tumultuous time of bodily and emotional change. I picture myself somewhere familiar to me, maybe sitting under a tree, and in my imagination, I see you, Lord Jesus, come and sit beside me and put your arms around me. I lay my head on your shoulder and open my heart to you and bring to you all those questions and emotions which others don't seem to understand or want to deal with. Somehow, your love and understanding, your forgiveness and encouragement heal, restore, and renew me. *(Pause.)*

I picture you, Mary, also coming and taking your place on the other side of me, putting your loving arms around me, and pressing me to your heart—filling up at that time in my life what I needed of a mother's and sister's love. *(Pause.)*

The years pass, and I see myself now as a young adult, venturing out into the world of work, of dating, or of the early years of marriage, the priesthood, or religious profession. Possibly, things didn't pan out as I had hoped and expected. There may have been disappointments or failures that discouraged, disheartened, or possibly frightened me and prompted me to doubt myself and distrust others. Whatever it was, Lord, I believe you know all about it. You

Appendix

were there through it all; you understand what no one else understands, and you can heal. I picture you coming to me at that lowest point in those years of my life, meeting me just as I am at that time, embracing me, and telling me: *"Though the mountains leave their place and the hills be shaken, my love shall never leave you nor my covenant of peace be shaken..."* (Is 54:10). You put me back together again, and, in the strength of your love and that of my mother, Mary, I can go on. I hear you say, *"Behold, I make all things new"* (Rev 21:5). *(Pause.)*

I recall now that particular event or area of my life that continues to haunt or trouble me. You know all about that too and can heal it. Like cancer under radiation, I bring it to you, the great Physician—to the light and warmth of your healing love. I picture you right there with me at the time—reminding me I was not alone. Your presence, understanding, forgiveness, strength, love, and peace fill me and restore me. *(Pause.)*

Lord, as I look back over my whole life, I want to remove all the blockages to your love and healing. I want to open all the doors and forgive everyone who has ever injured me or deprived me of the love or affirmation that I needed. I want to forgive parents, brothers and sisters, husband or wife, children, relatives, friends, teachers, priests, nuns, religious brothers, bosses or fellow workers, neighbors or schoolmates, fellow parishioners, and members of other races and religions. For all of them, and in particular for those who have hurt me the most, right now, by your amazing grace, I make the decision to let go of the resentment and to forgive. I begin to pray for them, asking you, Lord, to have mercy on them all, living and dead, as I beg you to have mercy on me. I know that, to receive your mercy, I have to be willing to extend mercy to others as well. *(Pause.)*

As I now open wide all the doors and windows of my heart and my memory to you, I let in the wonder of your light, your warmth, your love, your healing, and your peace. I hear the words of the prophet Isaiah, *"Consider not the things of the past. I am doing a new thing"* (43:18-19). I see myself like Lazarus of old, being called by name, called forth from the darkness and coldness of the grave to walk in the newness of warmth and love and light. I hear your words, *"Untie him and let him go...I am the resurrection and the life; whoever believes in me, even if he dies, shall live..."* (Jn 11:44 & 25). I also hear St. Paul's words, *"I live, no longer I, but Christ lives in me..."* (Gal 2:20). Lord, I want to die spiritually to the old self of sadness and sin and live anew. Live, Lord, in me and through me and make me a channel of love and truth, peace and healing to everyone.

About the Author
Msgr. Bob Guste

Msgr. Robert Guste, ordained in 1950, is a priest of the Archdiocese of New Orleans. He is from an old New Orleans family that has been actively involved in the religious, civic, and cultural life of the city of New Orleans as well as the state of Louisiana. Until his present ministry, he served in a number of parishes in the archdiocese for thirty-two years, affording him wide experience in suburban and downtown New Orleans, in the inner city, and in a small town area. He has been pastor of two congregations: St. Anthony's in Luling, Louisiana, for nine and a half years, and St. Francis de Sales, a predominantly African-American parish in New Orleans, for eight years. He was also administrator at Our Lady of Lourdes in New Orleans for about a year.

By choice and appointment of the Archbishop of New Orleans, since 1982, Fr. Guste has been working in a full-time ministry of evangelization and spiritual renewal. His ministry involves giving parish missions, retreats, days of renewal, and healing services. It also includes writing and a Monday through Friday radio program called "Living Waters" on WGCG, 600 on the AM dial at 6:30 A.M. Fr. Guste is also on world-wide short-wave radio 15.685 MHz on the dial every Monday through Friday at 10:15 A.M. Central Time.

Fr. Guste has traveled extensively in the United States and other countries and has taught and preached in East Malaysia and the Holy Land. He has also conducted retreats for Mother Teresa's nuns in Albania and other former Communist countries, as well as in Greece and the United States. He has been engaged in many movements for spiritual renewal, including the Christian Family Movement, the Cursillo Movement, the Third Order of Mount Carmel, the Catholic Charismatic Renewal, and the Jesus Caritas Fraternity of Priests. His community involvement has included work on behalf of interracial justice and correction reform, serving on the Board of Central City Economic Opportunity Corporation and chairing the Criminal Justice Commission of the Louisiana Interchurch Conference, of which he is still an active member.

Love's the Message that I Heard

He also devotes special attention to the cause of respect for life and participates locally in Priests For Life.

He is author of three other books, the first of which was on race relations, written during the integration crisis. The second, entitled *Mary at My Side,* is a personal testimony about discovering the reason and purpose of Marian devotion. His latest book, *The Gift of the Church,* affirms the need for and love of the Church. It addresses common objections and questions about the Church today. These books have been published by Queenship Publishing Co., Santa Barbara, CA. Fr. Guste is also author of a pamphlet entitled "Come Home to the Church," addressed primarily to Catholics who have drifted away.

Fr. Guste is presently in residence at Our Lady of Perpetual Help in Kenner, LA.

Other books by Msgr. Bob Guste available through
Queenship Publishing 1-800-647-9882

THE GIFT OF THE CHURCH
Msgr. Bob Guste

"Never in my lifetime, including over forty years as a priest, have I seen so many people who disconnect Jesus from His Church," says the author of *The Gift of the Church.* "To accept Jesus fully is also to accept His body the Church, for the Church is the continuation in a visible sign of the presence and ministry of Jesus among us today." If you love the Church, or if your love has gone tepid or grown cold; if you wonder about the need for the Church or question many of her teachings; if you have been hurt by members of the Church, disappointed in her or for any reason drifted from her fold, *The Gift of the Church* has been written for you. The book is full of honesty, faith and love. It could be a popular introduction to or companion of the new Catechism. It deals interestingly and readably with the everyday questions and attitudes people express: to go along with the institutional" Church! Why do I need the Church to guide me? Isn't the Bible enough? What about Confession; Mary; the Pope; contraception; etc.? This enthusiastic and hopeful volume could be used by R.C.I.A. programs, catechists, high school and adult groups, church book and pamphlet racks.

Order #3032 / $7.95

MARY AT MY SIDE
Msgr. Bob Guste

This sensitive volume is a heart felt personal testimony of experiencing a newfound spiritual relationship with Mary, the Mother of Jesus. *Mary at My Side* is for devotion to Mary. It is an evolving story of discovering in Mary significant and powerful help in fostering a relationship with her Son, Jesus. Msgr. Guste affirms an attention and devotion to Mary which has as its sole purpose being led to Jesus and ultimately to God the Father. With deeply moving frankness and simplicity, *Mary at My Side* portrays Mary as a prime example and model for all who are called to respond to Jesus in their lives. The book focuses upon the mystery and attraction of Mary within historical and contemporary expressions of spirituality. Special attention is paid to the impact of the traditionally accepted apparitions of Mary at Lourdes, Fatima and Guadalupe. Msgr. Guste also shares insights into the rosary and other prayer forms and devotions associated with Mary. *Mary at My Side* is welcome reading for those whose spiritual life involves the Mother of Jesus. It is also a book for the searching and the curious who do not understand Marian devotion or the place of Mary in contemporary Christianity. Lastly, it reaches out with a soft voice of intrigue to readers who otherwise usually find themselves antagonized by such devotion and attention accorded Mary.

Order #3031 / $5.95